Almost an Angel
by Deborah Michaels

Illustrations by Deborah Michaels

Almost an Angel

Trilogy Christian Publishers A Wholly Owned Subsidary of Trinity Broadcasting Network

2442 Michelle Drive Tustin, CA 92780

Cover design by: Grant Swank

For information about special discounts for bulk purchases, please contact Trilogy Christian Publishing.

Trilogy Disclaimer: The views and content expressed in this book are those of the author and may not necessarily reflect the views and doctrine of Trilogy Christian Publishing or the Trinity Broadcasting Network.

Manufactured in the United States of America

10 9 8 7 6 5 4 3 2 1

Library of Congress Cataloging-in-Publication Data is available.

ISBN: 978-1-63769-396-4

E-ISBN: 978-1-63769-397-1

Dedication

I dedicate this book to God, my heavenly Father, and my beloved family: my mother Marsha, my brother David, and my sister Susan.

Acknowledgments

First, I want to thank my Creator, God, who has blessed me every day of my life. Without Him, this book could never have been written. Thank you to my selfless Christian mother, Marsha, who edited my first draft of *Almost an Angel* and has loved and believed in me all my life. She gave me the idea of illustrating this book. Thank you to my dear devoted brother, David, for his technical support, encouragement, and sense of humor. Thank you to my sweet and loving sister, Susan, for her technical assistance and unwavering support. I also would like to thank the staff of Trilogy Publishing for going above and beyond in their pursuit of excellence in all areas of this book. Thank you especially to Mark Mingle for his kindness, valuable advice, and help in the publishing of this book.

Table of Contents

Foreword

To my dear readers: please read.

I want everyone who reads this to know that this is a work of fiction and is meant to be read as such. The Bible has never said that once we die, we can be sent back to earth for a second chance. In real life, God gives us plenty of opportunities to follow Him while we are alive on earth.

Also, I want to make it clear that Katie could never earn her way back to heaven based on her own merit. It is by God's mercy and grace that any of us could ever go to heaven. God is loving and forgiving. He let His Son, Jesus Christ, die on the cross so that sinful people like all of us are could still go to heaven after repenting and following his plan of salvation.

In this book, Katie is sent back to earth not so she can "earn" heaven but so that she has another chance to grow and become the Christian she was meant to be. In her previous life, she was a lukewarm Christian. Revelations 3:15-16 states, "I know your works, that you are neither cold nor hot. I could wish you were cold or hot. So then, because you are lukewarm, I will vomit you out of My mouth." Katie's spiritual mission is about her changing from a lukewarm Christian to one who is on fire for the Lord. It is important for her to grow her faith by learning to work for the Lord. James 2:26 says, "For as the body without the spirit is dead, so faith without works is dead also."

It is important for us to know how God says we can get to heaven so that we can share this truth with others. The following is God's plan for our salvation.

You must hear God's Word (Romans 10:17).

You must believe God's written Word (John 3:16).

You must repent of your sins (Acts 2:38).

You must confess Christ as your Savior (Matthew 10:32).

You must be baptized for salvation (1 Peter 3:21) and remission of your sins (Acts 2:38, 22:16).

When you are baptized, you are added to His saved, His Body, His church (The New Testament Church) (Galatians 3:27, Romans 6:3).

Living a faithful Christian life will then lead to eternal life (Revelation 2:10, James 1:12, Matthew 24:13).

Even after this plan of salvation, it is important to remember that it is only with God's mercy and grace that we go to heaven (Romans 5:15-17, 1 Peter 2:3). Romans 3:23-24 (KJV) says, "For all have sinned and fall short of the glory of God, being justified freely by His grace through the redemption that is in Christ Jesus."

In this book, I want to follow the Bible's teachings about becoming an active Christian while also demonstrating God's loving kindness, forgiveness, and grace to us all. I hope not only that you enjoy reading this but that this story helps you become closer to God.

Almost an Angel

Prologue

I will never forget that moment in time: the sound of the brakes screeching, my dad swerving our car. He was desperately trying to save our lives from a drunk driver as his gray truck careened across the lines, headed straight at us.

My mother glanced back at me, a look of horror on her face. Then there were screams. I think one of them was mine. And there was the shattering of glass.

It all happened so fast; yet, time also seemed to stand still. Suddenly, everything went black, and that was when I realized—I might be dead.

Chapter 1

I was floating through the comforting black space. I was free. My body was weightless, and I felt like I could fly. Then I looked up. There was this golden light, so beautiful that I wanted to go toward it.

I sensed an overwhelming feeling of love about me. The air was full of it. I looked down. Far below me, I could see the wreckage of our car. My parents, younger sister, and I were a bloody mangled mess in the wreckage of our blue minivan and the gray truck that had hit us.

Yet now, I didn't feel any pain. I looked down at my hands, my favorite Levi's jeans and black T-shirt—not a drop of blood was on them. I felt great, like a new person! If I had known dying was this easy and peaceful, I wouldn't have spent my entire life fearing and dreading it.

I kept on floating toward that golden light of peace, love, and forgiveness—God's light.

Then I saw a blonde man. He was in a long flowing white robe. My parents and sister were there, standing in front of him. My mother hugged me.

"Oh, I'm so glad you made it," she breathed a sigh of relief. "I didn't see you at first, so I wasn't sure."

"So," I looked at her in amazement, "we're dead?"

"I guess so. I never thought it would be so easy."

"Ladies, if I could have your attention." The loud, booming voice of the angel startled us into silence. "My name is Gabriel. Congratulations on completing your earthly life victoriously. I have keys to hand out to you. They open the door to heaven and to your mansion, which has been prepared for you."

Gabriel dropped the gold key into my dad's hand, my mother's, and then my younger sister's. I opened my hand when my turn came.

I closed my eyes, picturing myself in my own home, an eternal home; no dusting or cleaning, plenty of room to just be.

I opened my eyes. My hand was still empty. The angel held my key in his hand.

"Wait a moment." Gabriel held a white sheet in his hand. "Some instructions come with this one." He read the words softly under his breath. "Don't give this to Katie yet. First, she needs a chance to grow."

"Grow what? A pair of wings? I don't have to have wings to be in heaven. Just so I get my mansion, I'll be fine."

"I see what He means," the angel smirked at me. Who ever heard of a smirking angel? "You're not ready."

"Of course, I'm ready!" I argued. "I'm dead, aren't I?"

"Just because you're dead, it doesn't mean you're ready for heaven." Gabriel's eyes were stern as he gazed down at me.

"Does that mean you're going to send me down there?" I looked down, and there was only blackness, no light at all. I had never thought much about going to hell. My life on earth consisted of studying for final exams, dating, going shopping, attending church services with my family, and working at my part-time job at the university library. Now, *this* was the final exam, and I wasn't prepared.

"No. You wouldn't have made it this far if you were going down there."

"Oh, that's such a relief! You can go on and give me my key now," I smiled up at him.

"First, you must pass the test prepared for you."

"Oh, that's great! I'm a brilliant test-taker. I can recite the books of the Bible, the twelve apostles, and the Ten Commandments—"

"Silence!"

My mouth shut instantly. My cheeks burned with embarrassment. Was I really trying to impress a magnificent-looking angel with my piddling elementary collection of Bible knowledge?

"Listen."

He didn't have to tell me twice. He had my attention.

"You're going back to earth."

"Oh, I get it. Reincarnation, right? Can I come back as a princess this time?"

"Do you ever stop talking?" he roared.

I had always thought of angels as sweet little chubby cherubs who perched on your right shoulder and tried to talk you out of doing bad things. Gabriel was not one of those angels. He was fierce and instantly commanded one's attention.

"I'm listening," I replied in a small voice.

"You're going back to help someone. Hopefully, you will help yourself and grow at the same time."

"Oh, kind of like *It's a Wonderful Life*. Have you ever seen that movie? We watched it every—"

Gabriel glared at me. I stopped talking.

I looked around. I was all alone.

"Where's my family?"

"They've gone to their reward."

"That's it? I don't get to see them again? I don't get to say goodbye?"

"Oh, they'll be watching you, so try not to mess up."

"What'll I be doing?"

"You'll know when you get there."

"Will I have any special power?"

"For a while. But the longer you stay, the more human you'll become. So don't take forever performing your task. You'll have a special gift, but it will fade with time."

"How long do I have?"

"As long as it takes."

"That's cryptic! A month...ten days?"

"Enough! You will know when you've succeeded."

"And if I don't succeed?"

Gabriel looked at me sternly.

"I go to hell?"

Gabriel folded his arms and looked back at me. "That's not up to me. That's up to God."

I nodded meekly. Suddenly, my throat felt tight. "So, when does this start?"

Then all became black. I could feel myself falling, the sound of air whooshing in my ears. All of time had ceased to exist. I was neither in the past nor the future but somehow caught in space.

For an instant, the thought occurred to me that maybe God changed His mind and was sending me to hell instead of earth. Maybe the darkness around me was a part of hell. I shuddered at the thought.

Chapter 2

Suddenly, I broke through the earth's atmosphere. It was at night. Now, I could easily see the tops of the fluffy gray clouds. I looked up and noticed there was a full moon.

Then, I crashed through the clouds. I saw the twinkling lights of cities, neighborhoods, houses, and buildings.

Finally, I was being hurtled toward one tall building in particular. A man was at the edge of the rooftop, gazing down at the traffic below.

Suddenly, there was a crashing sound as my body slammed into his, knocking us both to the concrete floor of the apartment rooftop.

Strangely, I felt no pain. Then, I gratefully remembered that my "special power" must be kicking in. If I had been fully human, that would have hurt or even killed me! I laughed to myself. I kind of already was dead. I'd always had a morbid sense of humor.

"What in the world!" The man's voice shouted out from beneath me. He obviously didn't understand my sense of humor. The thought made me chuckle again.

"You think this is funny?" he glared at me. His eyes were silvery-blue. I could see them clearly, thanks to the full moon. "You come crashing out of the sky like a human cannonball and nearly flatten me to the ground. I can assure you I do not share your amusement."

"I never was graceful," I shrugged nonchalantly.

"Where did you even come from?" He rolled out from under me and slowly started to get up. "I was sure I was alone up here."

"I've learned nobody is ever really alone." I smiled at him, hoping my smile looked a little angelic.

When he stood up, I couldn't help but notice he was over six feet tall and had an athlete's build. His hair was thick, dark brown, and wavy.

I was sure he was my assignment. It would be so much easier if he was ugly because then I would never be distracted, and the truth is, I was terribly distracted.

Chapter 3

"What were you doing, hurtling out of the sky like that—like some kind of human bomb?"

I glared back at him.

"Yeah, I have a few questions of my own. What were you doing on a rooftop in the middle of the night—at the very edge, I might add? Were you sightseeing?"

The silvery blue in his eyes darkened to a stormier hue as his fury registered in them.

"That is none of your business."

"The devil loves it when you give up. You know, commit suicide? He probably has a special section down there for those who throw away one of the most precious things God has given them—their lives."

"Well, I don't believe in the devil."

"Oh, that's even scarier. He has more power over you when you don't believe."

His eyes were dark and suspicious as he studied my face.

"Why do you even care? I'm just another person. I don't even know you."

"Let's just say I have a 'vested interest' in you."

"I'm not in the mood for mysterious after the day I've had," he rolled his eyes. "What do you mean?"

"Just that you are my ticket back to heaven."

"What loony bin did they let you out of?"

"I'm telling you the truth. I'm going to sort of be like your guardian angel."

He turned around and laughed bitterly. "Of all the rooftops in all the world...she has to land on mine."

"Wow! You like *Casablanca* too? We about wore out our DVD of that movie."

"What's a DVD?" His face was puzzled. He was serious.

"What year is this?"

"Now, I know you're crazy."

"So, what if I am? I still need to know what year it is."

"1965."

"Oh, great! The Beatles are all alive!"

"Of course, they are! What are you talking about?"

"Never mind." I decided I better stop the "future" talk, or he would really think I was off my rocker. Oh wait—he already did.

"So, did you hit your head when you fell out of the sky? I can take you to the hospital. It seems as if you are suffering from delusions."

"I can assure you, sir, I'm fine. It would be in your best interest to listen to me and believe what I say."

"And I'm supposed to believe that you're some sort of angel, coming down to help me?"

"Well, almost an angel. That's where you come in."

"What am I going to do? Help you 'earn your wings'?" he laughed sarcastically.

"This isn't *It's a Wonderful Life*. If I don't succeed with you," I nodded my head toward heaven, "I might not get to go up there and join my family. They are waiting for me." Tears sprang to my eyes. "I already miss them so much."

His arms automatically went around me and pulled me to him. My tears made a big wet spot on his starched white dress shirt.

"I don't know who you are or why you're bonkers, but I always did hate to see a woman cry."

His kindness made me cry harder. I was weird like that, but I was really stressed out. I had no idea what to do in order to see my family again. Not to mention I had been thrown back in time to the year 1965. I thought of all the conveniences I wouldn't have: no computer, microwave, DVDs, or even VHS tapes. I wouldn't even have my cell phone—no wonder why I was crying.

He pulled out a pristine linen handkerchief and handed it to me. I blew my nose loudly into it and offered it back.

"That's okay. You keep it."

"It's just that I've never done anything like this before."

"What? You don't want to be my guardian angel?" His voice was soft, and his eyes twinkled.

"It's just that I'm not sure I can help you since I don't know anything about you. They didn't tell me a thing."

"Well, I guess that's all up to me then," he said. "My name is Charles."

His hand reached out and caught my hand in his. It was firm and strong. Then I stared into his eyes and found it impossible to look away. His eyes were deep, penetrating, and seemed to be looking into my very soul. After a moment, I realized my hand was still in his, and I snatched it back.

The corners of his mouth turned up slightly, and there was a look of amusement in his eyes. For some reason, that infuriated me. I narrowed my eyes at him and put on what I hoped was a stern face.

"This isn't funny."

"Who's laughing?" He stepped closer to me, his face inches from mine. I backed away, hoping he would follow my lead and do the same. Of course, he didn't. He just stood there, gazing down at me.

"Let me remind you that just a few minutes ago, you were at the edge of the roof about to jump to your death."

"Maybe I just needed a guardian angel to fall out of the sky and knock some sense into me."

"But you don't even believe in me!" I was totally failing at this heavenly mission.

"I believe that you believe you are an angel. Is that close enough?"

"Close enough...For now." I looked up at him with a little trepidation. This was going to be harder than I thought. The hugest challenge I'd ever had. The pressure was on.

Chapter 4

The sky had darkened while we talked. Clouds now hid the full moon. I couldn't even see Charles' face clearly anymore. It started to rain.

"Oh, no. My hair," I muttered automatically. Then I clamped my mouth shut and hoped he hadn't heard me. It was such a human thing to say. He'd never believe me if I kept making comments like that. I had to remind myself that issues like my hair just didn't matter anymore since I was dead.

He looked down at me and grinned.

"You sure do sound human to be an angel."

"Well, technically, I'm not really an angel."

"Oh, I'm so glad to hear you say that. I was hoping you weren't crazy."

"You didn't let me finish. I was almost an angel. I did die. Of course, when we die, we don't really become angels." I thought of Gabriel, the beautiful and majestic warrior. How different I was from a perfect being like that. I felt so much lower and insignificant.

"Okay. I'll play along," His voice broke into my thoughts. "So, what happens when you die?"

"Dying is easy. It's the living that's hard."

"Tell me about it. That's why I was about to jump."

"I can tell you now, that's not the answer. Life is temporary. Eternity is forever."

He rolled his eyes.

"Everything the Bible says is true. There is a heaven and hell. God is very much alive. There are real angels. When you die, you either go to paradise or hades (which is also called tartarus) until the Judgment Day. After the final judgment, you are then sent to heaven or hell. To go to heaven, you should obey God's commandments when you are on earth. You need to follow His plan of salvation, and even then, it

23

is only because of His mercy and grace that you go to heaven."

"So, what in the world happened to you?"

"I landed somewhere in between. I didn't quite make it to paradise. Gabriel told me I needed to 'grow.' Then I was sent back—to you."

"Lucky me." He put his arm around me protectively. "I'd better get you inside."

"Don't worry. The rain won't make me sick. I'm already dead."

"I wasn't thinking of just you," he laughed. "I'm still human. I could get pneumonia."

I looked away and smiled. It sounded like he was starting to believe in me. For some reason, that made me feel happy.

He opened the door on the rooftop and led me several floors down. The hallways were dim, so I couldn't see much. Suddenly, Charles paused at a gray, metal door, took a key out of his pocket, and let us in. He flipped a switch. Light flooded his apartment.

It was such a "guy's place," sparse but clean. He had a hideous olive-green sofa, easy chair, and love seat. I remembered that olive green was used a lot in decorating in the 60s and 70s. At least, Charles' décor was stylish for his time. The walls were a nondescript beige. The room hardly looked lived in, except for a bookcase.

"Are you hungry?" He was in his olive-green kitchenette. The counters were bright orange. The colors made me want to throw up.

"I don't know if I can eat."

"Because you think you're an angel?"

No, you idiot. Because your 1960s décor is making me sick, I thought to myself. Out loud, I said, "I just don't know if eating is possible for someone like me."

"We'll see. It can't hurt. How about a sandwich?"

"That does sound good."

"It's not like you're going to get a gourmet meal here, but I can definitely handle making you a sandwich. Do you like peanut butter?"

My stomach suddenly rumbled. Dying must have made me work up an appetite. "Actually, I inhale anything with peanut butter in it." It was one of my favorite foods in the whole world. I was so glad they had it in 1965. Now, if they just had good cheeseburgers, I was a happy girl.

He fixed us peanut butter and jelly sandwiches and brought them out to the living room. They were on white paper plates.

"It cuts down on my dishwashing," he explained with a crooked grin.

"But you have a dishwasher."

"I not only hate dishwashing; I don't enjoy loading and unloading dishes either."

I took a bite out of the delicious sandwich. I swallowed it and waited a few seconds. Yay! I didn't disappear. Looks like I could still eat!

"Do you have a place to stay tonight?" he asked.

"Not really." I hadn't even thought about practical things like that.

"Well, you're not staying under a bridge. After all, you did save my life. I have a guest room."

"Oh no, I couldn't."

"Do you have a better idea?"

"Uh...No."

"Then it's settled. You're staying here." He led me down a short hallway and opened one of the doors.

"It's small, but it's clean."

The walls were white. The double bed had a solid navy bedspread. The only other piece of furniture was a cherry wood night table with a small white ceramic lamp on it.

"Funny, this was an empty room until just a couple of weeks ago. I had no idea about what to do with this space. Then I decided to make it a guest room, even though no one has ever stayed here. I picked out the navy bedspread at Harrod's. It's almost as if I knew you were coming."

"That's either sort of serendipitous, or it's a little creepy."

"Maybe, it's a little of both," he laughed.

"I'll see you tomorrow, then?"

"Tomorrow, it is." He took my hand, touched it to his lips, and kissed it. His lips were soft, like velvet.

I snatched my hand away.

"I wish you wouldn't do that." I glared at him.

"As you wish, my darling."

"And don't call me that either."

I shut the door quickly in his face and locked it. Then, I put my ear to the door and listened to his footsteps as he walked away. Good. He was gone.

And I was alone to plot and plan on how to drag his sorry self to heaven and save myself at the same time.

Suddenly, I was deathly tired. I laughed. How fitting, when I was literally almost a corpse. Then, my thoughts turned serious again. The truth was, I had no magic plan to help Charles. But my plotting would have to wait. I was so groggy; I could barely stand. I practically fell into bed. Tomorrow was another opportunity to work on my mission. I had to make it count. I only had so many tomorrows left.

Chapter 5

I awoke to the smell of eggs cooking. The human side of me was very hungry. I walked toward the direction of the smell.

Charles was standing at his stove with a spatula over a frying pan. His white shirt sleeves were rolled up. He noticed me across the room and grinned.

"Did you sleep well?"

I nodded.

"I hope you like scrambled eggs. They are the only breakfast food I can cook."

"I like scrambled eggs."

I sat down at the little lime two-seat table he had right outside his kitchenette. He proudly handed me a plate of freshly cooked eggs. They tasted delicious. He had put cheese in them, just the way I liked.

"We really need to find your family. As much as I've enjoyed your company, I know you can't stay forever."

"Oh, so you are back to not believing in me."

"Your story is a little far-fetched, to say the least."

"Never mind then," I was getting testy. "You'll believe me someday. Right now, it's not relevant. I can still help you."

"You can start by not falling out of the sky and crashing into me again. I still can't figure out how that happened."

"I wasn't exactly in control at that moment. But—" I pointed out, "it did keep you from jumping off the roof."

"If you had my life, you'd want to jump too."

"What in the world happened? You don't seem like the suicidal type."

"I'm usually not. I just made a few huge mistakes. I got involved with a girl whose dad, I learned much too late, is part of the mob. She ran off with my former best friend, stealing a huge amount of money from her father. She said I did it, so now I've got a huge price on my head. I've been able to escape from her dad's hitmen several times already. But it's only a matter of time before they catch me. I'm a dead man walking."

"Wow. I'd jump if I were you too."

He frowned. "Thanks a lot. If you're an angel or whatever...I was hoping you'd have a solution."

"Let me think." I absentmindedly tapped my chin as I wracked my brain. I had never dealt with any problems of this magnitude before. Usually, my typical problem involved deciding on which jeans to get at the mall. This was more than a little out of the realm of my human experience. "We could either chase down your ex-girlfriend and try to reason with her, or we could get some money and pay off the mobster."

"How do you plan to get a ton of money like that? Money doesn't grow on trees, you know."

"Just how high of an amount was it?"

"Oh, maybe about a cool one million dollars."

I felt my throat tighten.

"A million?" That was a huge amount, especially for 1965.

"Unfortunately."

"You sure seem to have a knack for getting yourself into big trouble."

"Are you ready to jump ship yet? If you really are my guardian angel."

"That'll be the day." I may have sounded all breezy and confident, but I really wasn't. I had no idea how to help him and get that money back to his ex-girlfriend's mobster father. Then I remembered—I had a special power! Looks like it was time to go exploring through my bag of tricks and see what I had.

Chapter 6

It would have been nice if Gabriel had taken the time to tell me what my special gift was before hurtling me through the stratosphere back down to earth. However, since he didn't, I had to enlist Charles in helping me find out what it was. The first thing I wanted to test was my physical strength.

"Would you mind having an arm-wrestling match with me?" I asked Charles.

"What?" He was looking at me like I was crazy again.

"You heard what I said," I answered.

"What would be the purpose of that? I'm six foot two, and you are five foot two. Do you get a kick out of losing?"

"We'll see if I lose." I sat down at the kitchen table, put my elbow on it, and motioned for him to sit in the other seat.

He rolled his eyes and sat down reluctantly.

I grabbed his big, strong hand in my much smaller one.

"Okay. Ready, set, go!" I said.

Immediately, I was pushing his clenched hand toward my side. Then, as I watched him, getting red and starting to huff and puff, I felt a smidgen of pity for him. I even considered letting him win. But what kind of woman would I be if I didn't use the gift God gave me? I took his shaking hand and wrestled it down to the table.

"Unbelievable!" he gazed at me in shock.

"I believe the word you meant to say was 'congratulations.'"

"Oh...congratulations," he muttered. He shook his head in disbelief. "Do you want to try again? That must have been beginner's luck."

"Yes, I'm sure it was. Let's try again." My smile had an evil twinge. I was enjoying this.

We tried once more. And I won. Again.

"I don't understand. I was on the wrestling team in high school. I won trophies."

"It's not you; it's me," I said.

"What do you mean?"

"God must have given me superhuman strength for this mission."

"I don't believe you! And I really wish you would quit this guardian angel talk."

"That's all right," I said as I narrowed my eyes at him. "Someday, you'll believe me. How do you explain my beating you—twice? Especially considering my size." I looked at myself up and down. I had always been scrawny. Then I looked up at him inquisitively. His six-foot-two physique was massive compared to mine.

"There's got to be a logical explanation. Are you on some kind of drug?"

"Great! So, you'd rather think I'm a druggie than believe in a miracle?" He was such a pain.

"I don't believe in miracles. Everything happens by chance."

I shook my head in disgust.

"You are so wrong on so many levels." Why had God given me such a stubborn oaf to try and change? I didn't know if I could do this!

Then I heard Gabriel's voice in my ear.

"Anything is possible with God."

I smiled to myself. Why did I keep thinking I was in this all alone? God was with me and on my side.

But how could I make a million bucks suddenly appear before our eyes? Even Houdini hadn't been able to do tricks like that. During the last year of my life in the present time, I watched a documentary on the History Channel about Houdini. So, I really did know.

I racked my brain trying to think of a way to get that money. There had to be a way. Then my eyes sparkled. A solution was forming in my mind.

Charles was going to thank his lucky stars he had me for his guardian angel!

Chapter 7

I decided it would be dumb not to use the gift God had given me. What good was having superhuman strength if I didn't use it to help me during this adventure? All day I planned and plotted. I had even gone out shopping and bought an outfit to wear for the occasion. That night, Charles and I were dressed in solid black. I even had a black cap pulled low over my face. My hair was swung back into a ponytail. I thought I looked kind of cute and appropriately dressed for the job we were about to do.

I had Charles dress in a classy black turtleneck with black tailored slacks. I was startled when I first saw him that night. Dressed in that timeless attire, he could have been from any decade, even mine. He was very striking with his chiseled good looks and those silvery-blue eyes. I tried not to stare and looked down instead.

"We look like robbers." Charles glowered at me suspiciously. "I hope you aren't planning for us to steal money from some little old lady. That's where I draw the line!"

"Of course not!" I laughed nervously. "Do I look like the type to steal from little old ladies?"

"Appearances are deceiving, and I really don't know you that well."

"Then I guess you'll just have to trust me." I gave him what I hoped was a mysterious smile. "Could you please drive me to Tennessee Federal Bank downtown?"

"Why? Do you have some rich relative from whom you're going to steal a massive amount of money?"

"Stop arguing, and try doing what I ask." I snapped at him. It was Saturday night, so of course, all the banks would be closed. It was a brilliant time to do what I was planning.

Charles opened the apartment building door for me but then turned around. "You know, we could just stay in tonight."

I shook my head sternly and then gave him a little shove with my left hand that sent him stumbling out the door.

"Wow! You sure are strong to be so little," he muttered.

"Stop talking and go," I ordered.

As we drove, I enjoyed seeing Nashville in the 1960s. We were headed down 8th Avenue when I saw the older version of the Nashville skyline. Gone were the Batman BellSouth skyscraper and many of the others. The L and C Tower was there, surrounded by several smaller buildings. It was still Nashville, the city I loved and the home where I had always lived. There were no huge, towering condo high-rises. Office buildings were no more than three or four stories high. I asked Charles to drive me around several other streets downtown just for the fun of it. I saw people walking around window shopping at department stores like Harvey's, Castner's, and Cain-Sloan's. There were also several dime stores such as McClellan's and Woolworth's.

Finally, I saw the bank on Church Street. I motioned for Charles to park in the alley behind it. He slowed the car to a stop and then came around to let me out of the car.

"What in the world are you planning? I don't have a good feeling about this," he said.

"Be quiet and follow me," I replied between clenched teeth. I crept along the deserted alleyway. It was dark and scary. There were old tin garbage cans piled here and there. A cat from close by meowed, and I jumped.

Suddenly, I felt a man's hand on my arm, and I froze. Then I remembered it was Charles.

"It's all right. I'm here," he assured me.

"Shhh!" I whispered as I put my finger over my mouth. Finally, I saw the black metal door that was on the backside of the bank. I put my hand on the door.

Charles laughed. "What are you going to do—bust through the door?"

I narrowed my eyes at him. Then I turned the doorknob, and when I felt the resistance of the lock, I kept on turning until I broke it. The doorknob was loose in my hand. I opened the door.

Charles was tense and silent behind me. The fact that I broke through the door lock had shut him up. I smiled gleefully in the dark. The air inside was hot and humid. They must've turned off the air conditioner at night. I had instructed Charles to bring flashlights, and he clicked one on.

There were office desks in several corners and a counter at the front. I saw a big metal door in the back corner. I made a beeline for it. There was a round combination lock on the door. I ignored it and, without even trying, wrestled with the knob until I burst through the door.

Inside, there were mounds of money in neat little stacks with white paper around them. There was a large empty bag on the floor, lying there like an open invitation. I picked it up and began filling it with money.

"What are you doing? This is stealing! I never wanted to steal!" Charles protested.

"Oh, please. All of these banks are insured," I explained to him as I tossed money into the bag. "And if they're not, that's their problem!" It didn't take long to clean out the whole room. Charles wasn't much help. He just stood there, staring in horror.

I motioned for him to get out of there. He turned around, shook his head in disgust, and walked out. The money bag was probably about fifty pounds, but I swung it over my shoulder like it was nothing. I smiled triumphantly as I slipped through the broken back door and into the alley.

I laid the bag carefully into the backseat and then hopped into the car. Charles already had the engine on, and we roared off into the night.

"See, I told you this would work!" I said.

That's when we heard the police siren following closely behind. It was then I realized we were busted.

Chapter 8

I looked behind us. Blue lights were flashing.

"Uh, that wasn't supposed to happen." I felt a sudden pang in my stomach.

"Are you really supposed to be a guardian angel? My life is getting worse, not better," Charles muttered as he floored the gas pedal.

I checked the rearview mirror again. There was Gabriel sitting in the backseat, glaring at me.

"This is your idea of helping him?" Gabriel's arms were crossed over his massive chest.

I gulped. I felt like it was Judgment Day. "I was doing what I thought would help him most. I know you saw him about to do a skydive off his rooftop, but he's really not that suicidal. He just needs a little money to pay off that crime boss. Then he can go on his merry way."

"Silence!"

I was so engrossed in my conversation with Gabriel; I hadn't noticed Charles staring at me like I was nuts.

"Who are you talking to?" Charles asked.

"Would you believe it if I told you it was the angel Gabriel?"

"There's a hospital a few blocks from here where I could take you..."

"But you'll go to jail if I leave you now."

"At least, I'd be safe from the hitmen there."

"I won't desert you in your hour of need. At least, not yet, anyway," I reassured Charles.

"Pay attention, Katie!" Gabriel roared.

"I'm here! I'm listening." He didn't have to remind me twice.

"You need to change him from the inside out. Right now, he is a lost soul. He doesn't even believe in God. Throwing some money at him doesn't change his heart."

"Okay. I understand. I messed up today."

"Yes, you did, and you don't have forever to change him. Remember, the power you have will fade with time."

"Then why did you allow me to make this mistake today and waste that valuable time?"

"Hopefully, you *learn* from mistakes." His booming voice filled the car. I had no idea how Charles couldn't hear him. "Today, your mind was occupied with earthly matters, not heavenly ones. Charles is not the only one who needs to grow."

"I'm starting to feel like a failure."

"You have only failed when you won't try again."

"I'll do better next time."

"Good. Because I will be watching, and so will your family."

"Nothing like a little pressure," I said with a frown. "And what do we do about the policeman following us?"

"I'll fix this for you...this time." Gabriel gazed at me sternly, and then he vanished.

I looked up at Charles. He had been watching me intently the whole time, listening to what was to him a bizarre one-way conversation.

"What did Gabriel say?" His voice was teasing.

"Just that he'd fix this for us."

Suddenly, there was a gust of wind about the car. It blew harder and harder until it was like a raging storm. We could not see anything but swirls of gray wind around us. Even though I was already dead, I was terrified. Instinctively, I reached over for Charles' hand and gripped it tightly in mine.

Time seemed to stop as we spun around in space. It was as if we were in the very middle of the eye of a tornado. I had no idea where we were going, but I was scared to death.

Chapter 9

Suddenly there was a booming sound like thunder. It was as if someone had set Charles' car back on the ground. The wind slowly stopped swirling, and the air grew clearer. Charles and I were completely silent and still.

Then, the dust seemed to settle. I could see we were back at the parking lot of Charles' apartment building. I looked behind us. There was no policeman in sight. I breathed a sigh of utter relief.

Then I also remembered the money bag. I jerked my neck back in an instant to see if it was still in the backseat. It was gone!

Oh, no! All my scheming that day had resulted in nothing.

"You can't use money to fix your problems," Gabriel's voice whispered in my ear.

I almost answered out loud, "Why not?" but I kept my mouth shut. Better not to stir up Gabriel's wrath. He had already saved us once today.

"Well, that was an adventure," Charles said. He calmly took out a handkerchief and mopped the sweat off his face.

"How can you be so casual about this?"

"Someone has to remain calm! I'm sure there is a reasonable explanation for today's adventures."

"Such as?" I was curious as to his take on this evening's events.

"Did you put something in my scrambled eggs this morning?"

"What? You mean—like drugs?"

"That's exactly what I mean," he said, narrowing his eyes at me suspiciously.

"There's no way I would ever do that!" I said, opening my car door, then slamming it as hard as I could. His whole car shook. I started walking down the street, away from Charles—and everything. I needed a break, a little time for myself.

Soon, I heard his footsteps behind me.

"Don't leave," he said.

"Why?"

"You obviously need help. Maybe, I can find you a professional somewhere."

I kept walking, furious. Then I turned around. He was mere inches from my face. I backed away.

"You don't get it! You are the one who needs help! But you aren't cooperating!" I looked up. "I need a new assignment. Please don't leave me here with him!"

"You aren't getting a new assignment. This is it." The voice whispered in my ear.

"Great." I rolled my eyes. "I'm stuck with you."

"Good," Charles replied. "I didn't want you to leave anyway."

"Why in the world would you want me to stay? I nearly got you behind bars today!"

"My life is more interesting with you in it."

"Well, don't get used to me being around. I'm leaving ASAP."

"ASA what?"

I forgot—1965 lingo.

"*As soon as possible, dimwit!*"

"And now, even my guardian angel is calling me names. What is this world coming to?" His arms made exaggerated gestures in the air.

"In case you haven't noticed, there is very little about me that is angelic right now. So, you can stop calling me your guardian angel this second."

"But don't you want to save me?" His face was close to mine again. I looked into his silvery-blue eyes and was getting a little distracted.

"Stop that!" I gave him a little shove. "I'm not here for that!"

"For what?" he asked, grinning.

"You know what. I'm here to help you."

"Then help me." He was dangerously close.

"Not like that. I'm here to help save your soul, not your heart.

Once you've changed, I'll be gone."

"So, you keep saying—" he backed away then. "I'll be good. What happens next?"

"I don't even know you. I wish I did."

"They didn't let you see my entire life like Clarence did with Jimmy Stewart in *It's a Wonderful Life?*"

"That's my favorite Christmas movie. We watched it every year."

"It's my favorite too."

"Then why is it so hard for you to believe in me?"

"Movies are only make-believe."

"What is it that scares you most now?"

He turned away.

"I guess I'm afraid that I'll never believe in anything; that I'll never do anything worthwhile during my lifetime."

"I believe in God, but I think I was sent to you to accomplish something worthwhile. I was taken from earth before I could do anything spectacular."

"I don't consider saving me spectacular. Maybe, you should go back."

"Don't you see? If I don't help you, I don't help myself, and I might not see my family again. Why don't we become friends? You can start by telling me about your life."

"Do you really want to hear it?" He studied my face with an incredulous expression.

"I wouldn't ask if I didn't."

"Let me at least buy you dinner if you must listen to it all."

"It's a deal." We shook hands on it and then walked back together to his apartment. The mood was no longer romantic. It was more like two friends who had just realized they were on the same wavelength.

Chapter 10

I wanted to dress up for dinner with Charles. My black T-shirt and jeans weren't good enough.

I looked toward the closet and muttered, "Uh, Gabriel, could you please surprise me?" I shut my eyes and opened the closet door.

"You will have whatever you need when you need it." His beautiful voice danced in my ears.

I opened my eyes. Inside was an ivory lace A-line dress with cute lacy cap sleeves. It was the kind of dress I would have loved to wear when I was alive. It had that retro, old-fashioned look. So perfect for 1965.

I folded my jeans and T-shirt and put them in the closet. I wouldn't be needing them tonight. I took my blonde hair out of its ponytail and let it fall loose about my shoulders. My hair was long and wavy. There was a narrow rectangular mirror on the closet door. I looked at myself and wished I had some lipstick, powder, and—

shoes! How could I forget? I looked down at my sneaker-clad feet. I'd rather go barefoot than wear them with the ivory lace dress.

"Look in the closet again," Gabriel's voice whispered in my ear.

I opened it. It was full of 1960s clothes and shoes: peasant blouses, hip-hugger bell bottoms, tie-dye T-shirts, more A-line dresses, and even a pretty long blue dress with bell sleeves. It was a perfect clothes haven for a hippie.

At the bottom of the closet were several pairs of shoes. I was thrilled to see there were no high heels or platform shoes. I had always hated uncomfortable shoes. Then I remembered God knew me inside out, including all my preferences. I picked out a pair of brown leather sandals and put them on. They felt heavenly—which was fitting since God gave them to me.

There was also a blue makeup case next to the shoes. I lifted it up and set it on the bed. I couldn't wait to see what was inside. I opened the top. There were all my favorite makeup products: my foundation, eye shadow, mascara, peach blush, and powder, among other items...I was so excited! But my makeup also brought up flashes of memories—my mother and me having our "spa day" and experimenting with cosmetics; my sister and me going to Walgreens together, shopping for lipstick or mascara. Tears came to my eyes. I couldn't wait to see them again.

I put on my makeup. As I was digging through the case, I found one of my silver cross necklaces I had loved wearing at the bottom. I put it around my neck. My fingers touched the cross. Somehow, it made me feel close to God. It was nice to know that I wasn't all alone. Even after I tried to steal money to solve Charles' dilemma, God still loved me and blessed me.

I vowed to try harder than ever to help Charles and fulfill my mission. I went out to meet him in his living room.

"Wow! You clean up well!" he grinned at me appreciatively.

"Thank you."

"Where did you find the dress?"

"It was a gift." He might not believe me if I told him that it appeared magically in my closet.

I didn't tell him how good I thought *he* looked. He was dressed in a black tailored suit with a pressed white shirt and blue-striped tie. If I had spotted him on the street, I would have thought him a successful lawyer, doctor, or businessman. On the other hand, if I had lived in 1965, I would have been a fun, peace-loving hippie. I would have worn the tie-dyes, peasant blouses, and bell-bottoms, just like the wardrobe in my closet here. God knew my style so well.

Like a gentleman from Victorian times, Charles offered his arm to me. I took it. He opened the doors for me as we walked down the stairs of his apartment complex like I was some fragile piece of china. Then he opened his passenger car door for me. No man had ever treated me like that before.

He took me to Max's Steak House on Broadway in downtown Nashville. It was a glamorous white brick building with large Corinthian columns framing the front entrance. Two men dressed in black tuxedos worked as the restaurant's valet service.

I had never before gone to a place like this. The one or two boys I had dated before my demise were broke, and I was lucky if we went to Taco Bell or McDonald's. My family had been strictly middle class. Going to a meat-and-three was considered a real treat in my family.

The handsome valet whisked away Charles' car. Then the other man opened the restaurant door and welcomed us inside.

It was a vision of crystal chandeliers and low golden lights. There were lit candles at every round table. The tables were covered by white linen cloths that reached the floor. The floors were shimmery glasslike marble squares of white mixed with gray. Soft violins with a piano played in the background.

The maitre d' led us to a table in a secluded corner. Charles pulled out a chair for me. I ordered butter-glazed lobster with angel hair pasta. Charles got a filet mignon with whipped garlic potatoes.

While we waited for our dinner to be brought out, his face became serious.

"So, what do you want to know about me?"

"Everything."

"That would take all night, and I don't want to bore you to tears."

"Who says I'd be bored?" It was then that I realized that I couldn't wait to hear Charles' story, to know why he was so tortured and how he stopped believing in God.

Chapter 11

"Let me give you the condensed version..." and it was then that Charles told me the story of his life. For reasons that were unknown to Charles at the time, his mother had run off with her five-year-old son (Charles) and his two-year-old sister, Lydia, in the middle of the night, leaving their father behind. They travelled as far as their rundown old truck would take them, from Nashville to Wickliffe, Kentucky.

When their car had breathed its last, they went from farm to farm, begging for food and doing odd jobs. It was late fall, and the nights were getting colder. His mother got sick. There was no money for doctors or medicine, so she developed pneumonia. She died in Charles' arms in an abandoned barn. The police found him and his sister huddled together the next morning. They were shivering in the cold, their mother's corpse lying beside them.

The police tried to locate their father but were unable to do so. Since none of their family members could be located, Charles and Lydia were put in an orphanage. Lydia was sent to a foster home one year later. They had to pull her away from her brother's arms.

"Don't take her! She's the only one I have left!" he screamed. "I'll kill all of you!"

"Let her go, you stupid child!" The cruel female superintendent looked over her shoulder to her assistant. "Note that the boy has violent outbursts and tendencies. There's a reason he'll be staying with us."

That was the last time Charles ever saw his sister, but he vowed that someday, he would find her again, no matter what.

At school, Charles was bullied during his elementary years. The other boys would taunt him because they knew he was from the orphanage. He got into a lot of fights. It wasn't unusual for him to come back to the orphanage sporting a black eye and multiple bruises.

By high school, he had learned to take care of himself. No one bothered him anymore. He was over six feet tall, a hard worker, and studied every night. Now, instead of bullying him, his classmates respected him. He was never in the inner circle of the most popular kids due to his poor background. Instead, he was in a class all by himself—a bit of a loner who was perceived as quiet but very intelligent. He graduated near the top of his class and earned a full academic scholarship to Vanderbilt in Nashville, Tennessee.

Once there, he roomed and became best friends with Jeremy Stinson, the son of a doctor. Jeremy took Charles under his wing and taught him about the finer things in life: fancy restaurants, expensive cars, and how to blend in with society's upper crust.

They both majored in business and, after college, moved to New York and started a business together, renting limousines to celebrities and the affluent. They spent several years growing the business into a success.

Everything had gone smoothly until they met Angelina Moretti, a raven-haired beauty with an olive complexion. They didn't know much about her, except that she came from a very rich family.

Her father used their limo service constantly, transporting his daughter all over the city. She went to nightclubs, visited with her well-to-do friends, and made endless rounds to department stores and boutiques where she spent her father's money freely.

Although she was born with the face of an angel, her heart was far from angelic. She was fickle and very shallow. A huge stream of men had flown through her life. Some were bachelors, while a few were already married. She had no qualms about falling for men who were already taken.

She picked out Charles soon after she first met him. He wasn't a part of her wealthy circle of friends, but she really enjoyed the quiet and intense way his steely blue eyes followed her wherever she went.

Even when she wasn't looking at him, she could feel his eyes watching her whenever she was around him. Several times, she had caught him studying her in the rearview mirror. She decided it would be really funny to nearly make her father have a heart attack when she told him she was dating a limo driver.

One day she bluntly told Charles she was interested in him. He was stunned. Why would someone as gorgeous and rich as she was be interested in a limo driver? At the same time, he found he couldn't resist her.

She slowly pulled him into her depraved world of nightclubs, expensive drugs, and alcohol. It was mesmerizing at first. Then he eventually got bored with it and her. He didn't like the person he was becoming when he was with her and found her way of life meaningless. He planned to break things off with her.

What he didn't know was that by then, Angelina was already involved with his best friend, Jeremy.

One morning, he received a letter from Angelina:

Dear Charles,

I enjoyed the short time we had together. You are one of the few "good guys" I ever dated. This is why it hurts me to say this, but I am now seeing Jeremy. We have run away together. Breaking up with you hurts me much more than it will ever hurt you. You deserve someone better, and I hope someday, you'll find her.

Best of luck,
Angelina

Charles' head was whirling after he read Angelina's note. He hadn't even known when she had met Jeremy, let alone when they started dating. But girls like Angelina worked fast. He smiled bitterly to himself. It would be no time at all before Jeremy got a letter just like this when Angelina soon tired of him.

In a few days, Charles would have all but forgotten Angelina and her goodbye letter. However, he noticed he was being watched and followed everywhere by two burly, scary-looking men. They trailed his limo all over New York City.

After a few days of this, he grew so annoyed that he walked up to one of the men and simply asked, "Why are you following me?"

The guy seemed in shock that Charles had the nerve to ask this. That Charles didn't already know.

"Are you pretending to be that dumb, or are you that dumb? You owe my boss one million dollars!"

"Who is your boss?" Charles asked.

"Angelina Moretti's father, Ricardo."

"I don't owe him money! Who told him that?"

"Angelina did, you idiot! She left a note when she ran off with Jeremy, saying she was too scared to stay—since you had stolen a cool one million bucks from her father."

"That's a lie! I never stole any—" Charles started to say.

He heard the cock of a gun in the fist of the tall hitman, and he suddenly said, "Look—over there!" The men looked away a moment, and Charles ran to his car. He jumped in and locked his doors, and not a moment too soon. The two were beating on his window, and the tall one cracked his front side window with his gun.

Charles jerked his car out into the street and sped away. But he knew he wasn't safe. It would be no time at all before they found him again.

Chapter 12

Charles raced home to his tiny New York City apartment. He had to get out of town before Ricardo Moretti sent more of his goons after him. He was able to fit most of his clothes into one large suitcase. He threw them in as fast as he could.

Then he peeked through his blinds. There were two different men this time dressed in dark suits and matching hats, leaning against a parked car and staring up at his window. Even from his vantage point, he could tell the two men were built like rocks. That Moretti guy must have sent a whole fleet of men after him.

If he went out the front entrance of his apartment building, he was definitely a dead man. He went to the back of his apartment and quietly opened his window. There was an old rusty fire escape there. He might fall to the ground trying to get down that way, but it was his only chance.

He tried to be quiet as he went down, but each step seemed to clang and echo. Several minutes later, he was grateful to finally be on solid ground. He grinned, proud of himself for outsmarting another pair of thugs.

"Charles Montgomery?" A deep voice called from behind him.

"Who?" he asked. There was a pause behind him. That moment was all it took for him to get a plan. He swung his hard suitcase around and hit the big shady-looking goon in the face. The gun he held fell out of his hand to the ground. Charles dove for the gun, but so did the hitman. They crashed into each other, and Charles saw stars. He fought to stay conscious. If he couldn't, he'd never wake up again.

The massive dark-headed man wrapped his huge hands around the gun, but then Charles slammed his hands into the pavement. The gun fell to the ground again, free for the taking.

The other hitman wrapped his hands around Charles' throat. Charles jammed his elbow into the thug's stomach. He took the arms of the creep and flipped him over his back and onto the ground. He lay there, stunned and writhing in pain.

Then, the other one was crawling on the ground toward the gun. Charles stepped on his hand and kicked him as hard as he could in the head.

The man clutched his head in agony.

In a split second, Charles dove for the gun, threw it into a manhole, got his suitcase, and ran off. He decided taking his limo would be too dangerous since the mobsters had seen him driving it.

Fortunately, he hailed a cab almost immediately. He told the cab driver he'd give him an extra five bucks if he'd drive like a maniac and drop him off at his bank. They cut in and out of traffic. Horns honked loudly. Cars swerved not to hit them. The driver must have needed the money badly!

They came to a stop in front of Charles' bank downtown. He gave the driver a twenty-dollar bill and told him to keep the change.

CHAPTER 12

He ran in, closed his bank account as quickly as possible, and ran back out, stuffing several thousand dollars into his suitcase. He had another cab driver drop him off at the bus stop next to Central Park. Then he sat alone there as it began to rain. He had forgotten to take his umbrella with him. Rain fell on his hat and clothes until he was drenched. He wondered, wet and miserable, how his life could have deteriorated so fast. An hour and a half later, the bus finally came.

"Where are you going?" the bus driver asked him.

"Anywhere but here," Charles replied as he got on.

He sat down, staring blankly out the window. He truly didn't care where he went, just so it was out of New York City. He was done with that place. His other two limos were in an abandoned parking lot several blocks away. They would probably end up being towed somewhere. He didn't care.

He got on and off buses for two days. He was heading south. There was something in the South that felt safer than New York City, which had cold winters and sometimes even colder people.

He was homesick for the Southern way of life: people who asked how you were doing as you walked by, meat-and-three restaurants, and a slower pace of life. In his heart, he knew he wanted to go back to the last place he'd been completely happy: Nashville, Tennessee.

He planned to start a new life there: get a job, save up money to start another business, and find a place to call home. He soon found a nice clean, well-kept apartment on West End, near downtown.

He settled in, decided to take a few weeks off, and do absolutely nothing. During the day, he'd window-shop downtown, and sometimes he'd buy something for his apartment, like a coffee table or chair. He was slowly slipping into a peaceful routine. However, he couldn't help but wonder just how long it would last.

Chapter 13

On a Friday night in late August, Charles decided to go honkey-tonking downtown on Broadway and visit some of the bars in Printer's Alley. He wanted to relax and listen to some good country music. He wore a brown blazer over a white pressed shirt, a bolo tie, jeans, and brown leather cowboy boots. It was the perfect outfit for Music City, USA.

He went to the Black Poodle Lounge and listened to a young unknown starlet with a sweet, lilting voice. Then Dottie West and the Heartaches played, followed by Chet Atkins. At the end of the night, his stomach was full from the huge hamburger and hand-cut fries he had wolfed down. The country tunes he had listened to for hours kept replaying in his mind. He felt peaceful, happy, and safe.

He stepped out of the pub and walked down Printer's Alley toward Church Street, where the used red Ford Mustang he had bought two days ago was waiting in a deserted parking lot. The night was quiet and balmy for August with a cool breeze. Strangely, there weren't that many people out.

Suddenly, Charles felt the barrel of a gun against his back.

"Did you miss me?" The low menacing voice growled.

Charles jerked his body around. It was the tall thug from New York. His short but burly sidekick was there too.

"How did you find me?"

"That's our job. And may I add, we are good at it!" The tall one said proudly.

"If I had the money, I'd give it to you, just to get you off my back."

"So, you are finally admitting you took it?" The little one sneered.

"I don't have it because I didn't take it!"

"Our boss wouldn't have us following you if you didn't take it!" The tall man frowned grimly. "I must insist you come with us."

"What are we going to do? Take a long walk off a short pier?

Thanks, but no thanks."

In an instant, Charles reached for the gun, and then he and the large goon were struggling over it. Suddenly, the gun went off. The bullet ricocheted off the ground and into the shorter man's foot.

"Ow!" he yelped in pain. He doubled over and clenched his right foot. "Bruno, make him pay for that!"

Bruno and Charles still fought for control of the gun. Finally, it clattered to the ground. Charles kicked it into a street gutter.

"That was one of my favorite guns," Bruno grumbled.

"You shouldn't have tried to use it on me."

"What do you think we're here for, a picnic?" Bruno snarled again.

"I'll bring the sandwiches if you do dessert," Charles joked.

"Not funny," Bruno frowned.

"No sense of humor?"

"Not on the job. Never on the job," Bruno growled.

"Yes, killing isn't a funny business. Speaking of which—I am leaving now. Give your boss my regards. And no, I do not have his money. Why? Because I never stole it in the first place. Since you are now out of apparatus with which to kill me, goodbye and good night."

Having said that, Charles turned around and briskly walked away.

"Hey!" Bruno called out. "You think we're out of tools to murder you with? Think again!"

Charles turned around. There was a whooshing sound as a knife sliced through the air, aimed straight for his face. He ducked just in the nick of time. The knife missed him by mere inches and clamored to the ground a few yards away.

"And here I thought we could be friends..." Charles quipped.

"We didn't come here to be your friends," Bruno said grimly.

"Yeah, Charles, it's your fault I got shot in the foot," the little man muttered.

"Shut up, Jake," Bruno ordered.

"You wouldn't have gotten hurt if you hadn't been chasing me...

But there is time to learn from the error of your ways. Just go back. Tell your boss you never saw me, and we can all go about our merry ways," Charles told them.

"Boss already knows you're here. You're a dead man, Charles," Bruno told him. "If we don't kill you, someone else will. They won't be fun or nice like we are."

"Who said you were fun or nice?" Charles rolled his eyes.

"We are compared to the ruffians they'll send after you if we don't succeed in bringing you back," Bruno told him.

"Take me back where? New York?"

"Yeah, our boss wants to meet you. There are several options. If you can't pay him back, he said you could pay down your debt by working for him."

"How interesting! Sounds like a great job opportunity."

"Don't be so quick to make fun of his generous offer. He could just get it over with and kill you."

"So, I either become a hired gun like one of you gifted gentlemen, or I end up the cornerstone of the newest New York apartment building. What an option I have. Thanks so much, boys. I'll be awake all night trying to decide between those two choices."

"I informed the boss about how you can fight. My friends you beat up told me all about it. You could even be my new sidekick, while this one's foot—" he shoved Jake in the head "gets better."

"Hey, I thought you liked me!" Jake whined.

"Oh, pipe down." Then Bruno turned back to Charles. "Do you know of any doctors around here? Don't want this little one to get gangrene."

"I'm not so little!" Jake shot back.

"Well, I'm kind of new in town," Charles reminded them, "and haven't been to a doctor yet."

"You might need one if you keep refusing to work for the boss," Bruno told him.

"That'll be the day," Charles replied. "I'll take my chances."

"You've been warned. You're as good as dead. Wherever you go, we'll find you." His tone was chilling.

"Thanks for the warning. I'll be watching for you too." Charles turned around the corner of a building and disappeared from their view, walking toward his car. His mood since coming back to Nashville had been cheerful and positive. He was excited about the chance of starting a new life there.

Now, the possibility of that opportunity was going up in smoke. Feeling down and depressed, he knew he'd have to leave and hide somewhere else. Unfortunately, they'd follow him. "You're as good as dead." The words echoed in his mind as he drove home. His life was no longer his own, never living where or how he wanted. He rued the day he had met Angelina and fallen for her lies.

He went back to his apartment. He had planned on redecorating it to better reflect his taste, but now there was no point. He'd either be pushing up daisies or murdering old ladies to pay down a debt he never owed in the first place. What a swell life!

The minute he shut the door to his apartment, he felt claustrophobic. A wave of nausea surged through him, and his body swayed as his hand clutched his doorknob in order to steady himself. He suddenly had to get out of that apartment. The colors alone were enough to make him sick.

He went outside his apartment into the hallway and half stumbled up the stairs to the roof to get some fresh air. Once there, he stood still and stared at the stars.

"If there is a God, please help me. Please send someone—anyone. My life is in shambles, and I don't know what to do."

He looked up at the sky. The stars blinked back silently at him, almost winking as if they were making fun of him. What was he doing, trying to pray for help? No one was up there listening, and no help would be sent. He was all alone, as he had been most of his life.

And what a life it was, if you could call it that. His one and only friend had run off with his girlfriend, who got her mobster father after him. He had no friends, family, career, or even a city to call his own. He'd have to leave Nashville soon if he wanted to stay alive.

But that was the question—did he want to stay alive? He walked to the edge of the roof and gazed down into the peaceful darkness. It would be so easy to give up, to just let go. Dead people never got stressed out. He slowly stepped closer to the edge.

"And that's when you fell out of the sky and crashed into me, Katie..." Charles finished telling me about his life.

Our food had grown cold. I had been listening to Charles for the better part of an hour. Charles had our food sent back and reheated for us.

"So obviously, someone sent you to help me."

"By someone, do you mean God?" I asked.

"Whoever is up there."

"That's not good enough. Don't you see that it is a miracle that God sent me to help you and stopped you from killing yourself?"

"I guess."

"I'm leaving you right now if you can't see this. You'll just have to figure out your own mess."

"Then you might never see your family again."

"Good. Sounds like you believe part of my story, at least."

"I'm trying to."

"I wish I had some magic plan to fix your life, but I don't."

"Why don't we go home, get a good night's sleep, and start over in the morning?"

"Sounds like a plan."

After we had eaten, he got up and pulled out my chair for me and held out the crook of his arm. I put mine through it. I couldn't help but notice how well we fit together.

"And Katie?" he gazed down at me intently.

"Yes?"

"I'm glad you're here. I don't feel so alone anymore."

Chapter 14

We drove home in peaceful silence. The night was clear and beautiful, with the full moon still out. We were almost back to his apartment building. I was staring out my window, enjoying the ride.

Suddenly, Charles swerved around a corner.

"They're here!"

"Who?" I was jerked out of my thoughts.

"Moretti's henchmen."

"What are we going to do?"

"Get out of Dodge, that's what."

Charles was racing down alleyways, going the back way. He nearly hit a couple of trash cans; he was going so fast. He finally squealed to a stop in an alley two streets away from his apartment building.

"We're going to sneak up the fire escape, pack really fast, and get out of town."

"Where are we going?"

"I have no idea," Charles replied.

We walked quickly but quietly down the alleys. We didn't risk talking because they would be listening and watching for us. For all we knew, Moretti had a whole fleet of hired killers looking for Charles all over the city.

We tiptoed as fast as we could up the stairs of the fire escape at Charles' apartment building. After what seemed like forever, we were at the back door on his small balcony.

He got out his keys and was nervously fumbling with them.

"Don't drop those. They'll hear us," I whispered.

"I know. I'm just looking for the right key, and I can't find it!"

"Let me see if I can open it," I said.

"How are you going to open it? You don't even have the key."

"Just get out of my way." I gave him a little shove and put my hand on the doorknob. I desperately hoped it would work. I twisted the knob in my hand and heard the lock give under my pressure. The door swung open.

"How'd you do that?"

"Special power. Remember? Unfortunately, it's on loan to me for just a limited time."

"Well, it sure comes in handy," Charles said gratefully.

We didn't dare turn on the lights. Luckily, the curtains weren't drawn in our bedrooms. The bright moon gave us a natural light so we could see what we were doing. Gabriel must have known we would be leaving. There were two gorgeous brown leather suitcases on my bed.

"Thank you," I mouthed as I looked up. Then I opened the suitcases. They were empty. "You didn't pack them for me?"

"Don't be lazy," Gabriel's stern voice warned in my ear.

"Sorry." When was I going to stop being so human?

I crammed all my clothes in the suitcases and was barely able to get everything in. I took my cosmetic box too. No matter where we went, I still wanted to look good.

I walked out into the living room, thankful that it was too dark to see the ugly decor for the last time.

I had one suitcase under my arm balanced on top of my other suitcase. I held the handle for my makeup box in my other hand.

Charles only had one suitcase of his own to carry. In the moonlight, he gazed at me and smiled, clearly amused.

"Do you need some help carrying those?"

"Yes, that would be much appreciated," I admitted.

"You sure have a lot of stuff for a guardian angel," he smirked.

"I hope you have plenty of space in your trunk." I was a little embarrassed. I must seem so human to him to have been sent from heaven.

"I do. Come on—they could be coming any minute!"

We didn't use the fire escape this time. It would be awkward to carry the suitcases that way with the rickety stairs, so we started to run down the hallway.

As if on cue, we heard them crashing down the hall. Gangsters were so loud!

We hid around a corner but heard them as they busted down Charles' door and shot up his apartment. At least, someone would have an excuse to redecorate now!

While they were busy target practicing in the apartment, we made a break for it. We raced toward the back door. It led to a stairwell all the way to the bottom floor.

I was doing fine with my superhuman strength lugging my suitcase and cosmetic box. Halfway down the seven flights of stairs, Charles was huffing and puffing.

"What did you put in here? Bricks?" He managed to mutter.

"I only stuffed half my wardrobe in there. Here, let's swap." I handed him my lightweight box and reached for my heavier suitcase.

"I can't carry a cosmetic case! It isn't exactly manly."

"I'm not going around without makeup. Anyway, who cares what people think?" I rolled my eyes. "Just take it!"

He grumbled something under his breath but took the small case, and we started running down the stairs again. In just a couple of minutes, we were on the ground floor, and then we ran out the back door. A barrage of bullets met us as we scrambled across the open space between the apartment building and one of the alleys that led to Charles' car.

"Run in zigzags—" Charles yelled. "It'll be harder for them to hit us."

"Don't worry about me," I yelled. "I'm already dead! You run in zigzags!"

He must not have believed me about my already being dead because he put my makeup box in his left hand that already held his suitcase and grabbed my wrist with his other hand. So, I was forced to follow him as he zigzagged his way across the open pavement. The killers probably thought we were idiots. All the time while we were running, bullets whizzed past our ears and ricocheted off the ground. The thugs were standing on the fire escape outside Charles' apartment, obviously aiming every bullet they had left at us.

We finally dashed around the corner of another building, out of the line of gunfire. Then we ran down the alleys to find his parked car.

"Hurry! They'll be following us!" Charles managed to say as we ran.

"Well, duh!"

"What?" he gave me a puzzled expression.

"Never mind." They must not have used that expression in the 1960s.

Since it was the middle of the night, no one was out but us and, obviously, the thugs. A dog howled in the distance, and the moon cast a silvery glow about us. It's funny the things you notice while you're running for your life, or in this case, Charles' life.

Finally, we made it to the car. He opened the trunk, and we threw the luggage in, jumped in the front seat, and roared off.

"Wow! What an adventure!" I said between huffing and puffing. I had never done anything like this before.

"Yeah. It's so much fun being shot at," Charles muttered.

"So, where are we going to go?"

"Out of Nashville. Somewhere they won't find us."

"Is there such a place?"

"We're about to find out."

We drove in peaceful silence, heading out of Nashville, going north. We passed by what would later be the beautiful skyline of Nashville. Right now, however, the red letters of only the L and C Tower blinked back at me, surrounded by just the several shorter buildings.

We were soon out of Nashville, headed toward Clarksville. Dark black forest surrounded us on both sides. It looked like we were in the middle of the wilderness, except for the road we were on. After a while, we were on the other side of Clarksville and driving toward Kentucky.

I yawned.

"Are you tired?" he asked.

"Well, it is about 3:00 a.m."

"I've got a shoulder you can rest on," he said. He stretched out his right arm until it was securely around my shoulders. I scooted over toward him but shot him a wary look.

"All right...just so you remember, we're only friends."

"Don't worry. I'll be on my best behavior. Now, stop talking, and just rest."

I smiled and closed my eyes. I felt so safe around him. Yet I was supposed to be the one here saving him. I fell into a deep and dreamless sleep for over an hour. Suddenly, the car swerved, and my eyes flew open.

"What's wrong?" I asked. Could the mobsters be after us again so soon?

"Look..." he replied, nodding his head toward the middle of the road.

There was a young mother there waving her hands wildly for us to stop. Charles had barely missed hitting her. Her two young children, a boy and his younger sister, were huddled on the side of the road, clinging together in terror.

When she saw we were going to stop, she ran to the driver's window. She was probably in her late twenties, with thick auburn hair pulled back into a ponytail. She had a black eye, and blood dribbled down the side of her mouth. Charles quickly rolled down his window.

"Please help us!" she cried out, "—or he will kill my children and me!"

"Who?"

"My boyfriend! He's drunk again!"

"Where is he?" Charles' jaw had grown tight.

"In the house."

"I'll be right back. You and the kids get in the car."

Charles strode toward the house with a steely determination in his steps.

I nestled the mother and her two children into our backseat. Then I got a blanket out of the trunk and put it over them.

"Thank you," the mother said with tears in her eyes.

"You don't have to thank me. I'm just glad we were here. You stay in the car while I go see if Charles needs help."

I hopped out of the car and ran like crazy toward the little log cabin where he had already disappeared. I knew that sometimes drunks could possess the strength of ten hardy men, and I had to make sure Charles didn't get killed this very night.

Chapter 15

The door to the cabin was open, and I let myself in. The cabin was in complete disarray. Glass dishes and pictures lay smashed on the floor. Furniture was turned over, and there was food, probably soup, dripping off one of the walls where the drunk had thrown it. There was an eerie silence at the front of the house. But as I walked toward the back door, I could see two black figures struggling in the dark outside. I went through the house, looking for a weapon. In the kitchen drawer, I found a large serrated knife. I also grabbed a large glass vase from the counter, one of the few breakables that wasn't already destroyed.

Then I ran out the back door, looking like a madwoman clinching a knife in one hand and a huge vase in the other. I shouldn't have worried so much. Charles was on top of the drunk, pummeling his face back and forth like a punching bag.

"If there's one thing I hate, it's a man who beats up women and children!" Charles managed to say as he was hitting him. The drunk wasn't even responsive, and there was blood already streaming out of his nose.

"Come on, Charles. You're going to kill him—" I put my hand on his shoulder.

"Good."

"Not good. You'll be sent to prison for murder. It isn't self-defense anymore. Good job! You've put him out of circulation." I gave him my hand to help him up. "Let's go. He won't be hurting anyone else tonight."

He got up. Then he took a good stern look at me. "What are you doing with that knife? You're going to hurt someone. Here, give it to me." He took the knife and threw it into the dark bushes.

Suddenly, the drunk got back up and put his hands around Charles' neck in a vise-like grip. He started to drag him backward as his hands wound tighter and tighter around his throat. He turned away from me, but I saw his shoulders tense as if he were putting all his strength into strangling Charles.

I looked around in a panic for the knife that Charles had so nonchalantly tossed out a moment ago. It was nowhere in sight. Rats. Then I remembered as I looked down. I still had the vase!

All of the drunk's efforts and attention were on strangling Charles to death. I could hear him gasping for air, even as he was trying to flip the drunk over.

I took a few quick steps, trying to be as quiet as possible until I was right behind the drunk. I held the vase high in the air and then smashed it over his head. I put all my extra strength into it, and the glass shattered into smithereens. Pieces of it were embedded in his scalp.

He keeled over as his hands fell from Charles' throat. His eyes rolled to the back of his head as he lost consciousness and fell to the ground.

Charles was hunched over, coughing and sputtering. When he was able to breathe again, he surveyed the damage my vase had done.

"You may have killed him."

"Good. He deserved it. He was going to kill you."

"Yes, I'm well aware."

"You didn't make it easy on me, hiding my knife."

"Looks like you didn't even need it," Charles grinned.

"I do what I can." I wondered if he could see my eyes sparkling in the dark due to his almost-compliment. "By the way, why were you so engrossed in using his face as a punching bag?"

"He reminded me of what my dad must have been like when my mother ran away with us. I can't stand a man who is violent with women and children."

"Did your dad beat you?"

"I don't know. Thankfully, I was too young to remember." Then he gave the drunk a nudge with his foot. "Yeah, he's going nowhere else tonight. He's either dead or he's going to have a major headache when he finally does wake up. Let's get out of here."

He took my arm as he gingerly stepped over the drunk's body. We walked back through the house and shut the front door. When we got back to the car, we found the mother and her two children still hiding in the back seat, looking petrified.

"We're going to the police. Where are the police in Paducah?" Charles asked.

"Why are we going to the police? They ain't gonna do a thing," the woman told us.

"What do you mean? Have you tried going to them before?" I asked.

"He's been put on probation three times already. He even spent a night in jail. It doesn't do no good. They always let him out, and he comes back home. Each time, he promises things will be different, but they aren't. Ever."

"Then we'll find you a safe place," Charles promised. "I'm thinking of one right now where no one will find you."

The woman introduced herself as Paula. She had been married several years ago to a very kind man, but he had died in an accident at the factory where he worked. Then she had wound up with her current boyfriend for two years. He quickly turned into a drunk louse and told her he would kill her and the kids if she ever left him. Tears flowed freely down Paula's face as she recalled the many times she had tried to get help from the local police. Charles was clearly steamed as he listened quietly. I felt like crying myself, listening to all that she had been through. She then settled back into her seat and closed her eyes, clearly drained from everything that had happened.

Charles drove us along the back roads of Kentucky. It was dawn, and there were orange and bright pink shades of color shooting across the sky in the East, beside us. I studied the scenery of Kentucky in the morning light: beautiful, old, dilapidated barns you could see the sky through, quaint farmhouses surrounded by fields of crops, even some goats and sheep. There weren't even any towns around.

We took a turn down a dirt road. A few miles down the way, there was a sign that said, "Lovelaceville, population 102." There were a tiny gas station and a general store. Charles was right; no one would ever find them here.

"But where would we live?" The woman asked. "I don't even see any houses."

"Just wait. I'm sure we'll find one." Charles looked at me. "Do you think they—" he glanced up, "could help?"

"I'll get back to you on that," I said nervously. I squeezed my eyes shut and started silently praying like crazy. *God, please help this poor single mother and her children find a home. She needs a place to start a new life. We've done all we can do for her, but now we need a miracle. Thank you. In Jesus' name, Amen.*

I opened my eyes. "Turn left," Gabriel's voice said softly in my ear.

"Turn left!" I shouted.

The brakes squealed as Charles suddenly jerked the car to the left. There happened to be a dirt road there that seemed to appear out of nowhere. Tall oaks and tulip poplars met over our car so that when you looked up, you could barely see the sky.

We drove on for about another half mile. I was beginning to think Gabriel had played a trick on me, but then there was a clearing. I saw an old rambling farmhouse with a "For Sale" sign out front.

"That's it, Mommy!" the little boy squealed. "That's where we are going to live!"

"Yeah, that's it," I murmured under my breath and smiled. When was I going to learn that God would never let me down? As we got closer, I saw it was in a state of disrepair. Some of the shingles had fallen off the roof. The house itself could really use a new coat of paint. One of the windows had been broken—and that was only on the outside.

Uh, Gabriel? This isn't exactly in move-in ready condition. We don't have time to help them fix it up. Could you send us some help? I said to him in my thoughts.

"Nonsense. You have nothing but time. Don't be lazy. The mobsters aren't going to find you here any time soon. You're literally in the middle of nowhere. You can't stay here forever, but you do have time to help them," Gabriel told me.

But I'm terrible at repairs and fixing up houses! I hate to even chip a fingernail, I thought frantically.

"It will be worth it. You'll see," was Gabriel's answer.

But—

"No buts!" Gabriel's voice thundered in my ear.

"Okay," I muttered under my breath. I glanced up, and Charles was studying me with a puzzled look on his face.

"Who are you talking to?"

"You don't want to know," I replied.

Charles smirked. Maybe he was getting used to my weird ways.

"So, are you going to just leave us here?" Paula asked. "We don't have no money left to buy that house."

"You don't need money to buy that house," Charles said warmly.

"What? Why not?"

"Because I am going to make a down payment on it."

Tears sprang to Paula's eyes.

"Why would you do that? We are strangers, nobodies that you just met."

"There isn't any such thing as a nobody in my book. Besides, you are no longer strangers to me. I've already been up close and personal with your boyfriend, who nearly strangled me to death. Plus, you've been riding in my car half the night."

"We could never accept such a huge gift from you. What kind of person would that make me?"

"A smart one!" I piped in. "If I was with that animal, I know I'd want to get away!"

She laughed through her tears.

"Please don't say no," Charles said. "It would be a privilege to do this for you and your family."

"Well, when you put it that way," Paula beamed, "I guess it's okay."

When Paula smiled, I could tell she must be really pretty without her black eye, bruises, and swollen face. She was pale with delicate features and was a cute petite size. Then a thought occurred to me. I wondered if Charles could fall for a woman like her and if they could be happy together. Then those two little kids would have a loving father to raise them. I put the thought in the back of my head for a later time, but the wheels were already turning.

Chapter 16

Charles stopped at the one gas station in town. It was a quaint two-story building straight out of *The Great Gatsby*. The top floor was obviously used for living space. The gas pumps outside were painted in a bright shiny fire-engine red. The place had a cute retro feel. Even in 1965, it looked like it was from the 1920s.

There was a grisly long-bearded man working the cash register. He viewed us with dark, suspicious eyes, not saying a word. Apparently, his customer service skills were lacking.

"Hi there," Charles said in a warm voice. "There's an old house down the dirt road about half a mile from here, and it's for sale. Do you know who owns it?"

"Why do you want to know?"

"Because we would like to buy it today."

He looked Charles up and down and then frowned. "Why

would a man like you want a house like that? Shouldn't you be in a penthouse somewhere like New York?"

Charles shook his head awkwardly. "It's not for me. It's for a friend."

The man glanced at me and then let out a knowing laugh. "Oh, I see. You're trying to set up your mistress here at an out-of-the-way destination. Well, we don't do things that way here. This may be the boonies, and we may be old-fashioned, but—"

"You totally misunderstood!" Charles interrupted.

"I'm not his mistress!" I had to put in my two cent's worth.

"Oh, so you're just buying the house for your pretty little sister?" The man rolled his eyes. "I wasn't born yesterday."

"I don't know what you're thinking, but none of it's true! This house isn't even for me!" I bristled at this ignoramus.

He stretched his neck and looked over our shoulders, seeing Paula with her two kids in the car.

"You have two mistresses and one with two kids? You've been a busy man!" The old-timer narrowed his eyes at Charles. "Are you a mobster with a girlfriend in every port?"

"Before you pop a vein in your neck or drop dead from a heart attack, I'll have you know that I am single, and neither of these ladies is my mistress! I don't know how much plainer I can be. Do you want a signed affidavit?"

"A what?"

"Never mind." Then Charles turned to me. "Maybe, we should take our business elsewhere. This might not be a good place for Paula and her two children to live after all."

We opened the door to leave.

"Wait!"

Charles and I turned around.

The man's face was red with embarrassment. "I'm sorry for not believing you. It's just that hardly anyone comes to Lovelaceville unless he's lost or something shady is going on. We're not used to strangers."

"Obviously," Charles murmured under his breath, where only I could hear. Out loud, he said, "Then let's not stay strangers. I'm Charles Montgomery. This is Katie, and that's Paula with her two children out in the car. Paula needs a new start. That's why we'd like to get her that house, so she can raise her children here. Now, can you tell us who owns that house so we can contact them?"

"My name is Sam Wilkes, and actually, I own that house..." the man said quietly. "So, she needs a new start, eh? Don't we all!" Then he let out a big barrel laugh. "How much you want to pay for it? I know it's not in the best condition."

"I have cash. Would you take a $500 down payment?" Charles asked.

"$600, and it's a deal." Sam offered.

"Done!" Charles shook Sam's hand heartily.

"Just one thing, though...why in the world would you carry several hundred dollars in cash?" Sam's eyes still had a suspicious glint in them. "You aren't on the run from the law, are you?"

"I've done nothing recently to break the law," Charles told him. "I can assure you; the law is not after me."

"But someone is. No one carries that amount of money around for the fun of it."

"I mean this in the nicest way possible. Take the money, and don't ask questions." Charles' voice had grown steely.

"All right. I'll take your money, but if it's counterfeit, I'll be the one coming after you."

"That won't be necessary. Everything is legal that we've done today."

Charles went back to his car and got the money out of his suitcase. He brought it back to Sam. They spent at least twenty minutes counting it down to the last dollar. Then Sam reached behind the counter and gave Charles the title to the house.

"Thank you, Sam," Charles said cheerfully as we walked out the door. "What a grouch!" he muttered when we were out of earshot.

"Yeah, but you got what you wanted, all the while staying a gentleman," I reminded him.

"I didn't feel like a gentleman. I felt like slugging the guy."

"Why don't you pray for him? You can't hate people you pray for."

"Why should I pray for him? I hate the man. Cursing him is more like it."

"The hate you feel only hurts you. The man back there couldn't care less how you feel. So, the anger only festers inside of you like a cancer. Praying for him changes how you feel. It puts things into perspective."

"I don't know how to pray."

"Why don't we practice tonight?" I offered.

"I don't know."

"Are you afraid?"

"That'll be the day," he growled.

"Then meet me tonight at 9:00, and we'll try it together." I wondered what he'd say, scrunching my toes together. But how could I be a proper guardian angel and not try to help save his soul?

"I'll try it." His voice was so low; I could barely hear him.

"You will?" I beamed. I twirled around in the light of the sun. I felt like dancing in the air. I was so happy. This was the first hint of spiritual progress I'd made with him.

He threw up his hands in defense.

"Hey, I only said I'd try."

"Don't you get it? That's all I ask—only that you try!"

Chapter 17

"What are you two so happy about?" Paula asked as we walked back to the car.

"Charles—" I started.

"We got the house!" Charles interrupted with a big grin on his face.

Paula was practically jumping up and down in her seat. Her two children squealed with delight.

"You mean I've got my own home?" Paula shook her head in disbelief.

"Not only that, we're going to help you fix it up!" I told her.

"We are?" Charles muttered under his breath. I elbowed him to shut him up.

"Thank you so much!" Paula was crying again. "I don't know what I ever did to deserve this!"

"Dry those tears! We're going to have fun! I've never decorated a house before!" I was no longer dreading helping Paula with her new home. Now, I was so excited I could hardly wait. The most I'd ever gotten to decorate was my college dorm room and my bedroom at home. Charles shook his head and rolled his eyes.

We all got back in the car and drove to an adorable, sleepy little town called Wickliffe. We checked into a small motel. Paula raised her eyebrows when Charles booked three rooms: one for himself, one for Paula and her children, and one for me.

"I thought you two were married!" she said.

"Of course not!" I shot back.

"But you are together...right?"

"We are good friends," Charles broke in.

"Oh, okay." Thankfully, Paula was smart enough to drop the subject like a hot potato. I don't know why people kept assuming we were a couple. That was more than a little awkward.

We all went to our own suites and slept most of the day. In the late afternoon, we got up and went shopping for things that Paula and the kids would need, like mattresses, linens, furniture, and groceries.

Charles hired two of the local Wickliffe men who had big trucks to follow us back to Lovelaceville. The backs of the trucks were piled high with mattresses, wooden chairs, and a round maple kitchen table we had found at a second-hand store.

We went like a mini caravan back to Paula's new home as it was getting dark. Sam had given us the keys earlier that day. We couldn't wait to start making that house a home. When we drove into the dirt driveway of the house, a lovely sight met our eyes. There was golden light spilling out of every single window, almost like the house itself was calling out to us, welcoming us into her folds.

Paula's two children, Jessica and Aaron, jumped out of the car and ran toward their new home, laughing and yelling. It was hard to believe that just a short time ago, they had been terrified for their lives and for that of their mother's. Kids were very resilient.

"I can't believe it!" Paula squeezed my hand. "We're going to be so happy here!"

We walked up the steps to their new home. A portly, jolly middle-aged woman met us at the door. She had a basket with freshly baked corn muffins in her hand. Jessica and Aaron ran up to her, and she gave each of them one.

"Thank you, ma'am," Aaron said in his little five-year-old voice.

"You are more than welcome, honey." She told him as she patted him on the back.

The delicious smells drifting from the kitchen made my stomach growl.

Charles must've heard and looked down at me and smirked. "So human," he whispered. I elbowed him again.

"I took the liberty of making you some beef stew for your first night here," the kind lady told us. "My name is Ethel Wilkes. I'm Sam's wife. You are going to be our new neighbors. We live right down the road from you, about five cornfields away."

"You're Sam's wife?" Charles seemed shocked that Sam would have such a sweet wife.

I walked as if in a trance toward the back of the house, following the smell of the stew. I felt like a rabid animal almost foaming at the mouth; I was so hungry. When I got to the kitchen, I noticed the ugly yellow-flowered wallpaper was hanging by shreds in some places. It would definitely need to be removed. Then my eyes focused on the stove, the source of the yummy smell. There was a huge pot chock-full of chunks of beef simmering in red sauce with pieces of onion, corn, and noodles. And there was a stack of brown Melmac bowls on the counter, with a ladle and spoons beside them.

"I thought ya'll might be hungry tonight," she said. Ethel's loud voice made me jump. She was right behind me.

Hungry was an understatement. Evidently, beating up a drunk guy made me ravenous. Ethel went around me to the stove and ladled out thick stew into each Melmac bowl.

Charles and the other men quickly unloaded the kitchen table and chairs so we'd have somewhere to eat.

"Donny and Tom, do you want to eat with us too?" Charles called out to them.

"Thank you, man. We're starved." Tom answered. The other man nodded his head in agreement.

So, we had this odd assortment of almost strangers and people we had just met.

"Why don't we hold hands and give thanks for this great meal?" I suggested.

It seemed awkward at first as everyone reached for the hands of the people beside them, but a strange peace suddenly settled about the room as we bowed our heads.

"Lord, thank you for this delicious meal Ethel has prepared for us. Thank you for her kindness and generosity. And thank you for this beautiful home, and please help Paula and her children to be very happy here. In Jesus' name, Amen." I wasn't into long prayers when I was praying in front of a bunch of people. Plus, the kids would be squirming in their seats if I went on too long.

Dinner was so much fun. We talked about what colors we wanted to paint each room. Ethel apologized for Sam's behavior this morning. It turned out that he had been in a deep depression since his son was drafted into the army in the Vietnam War. Paula gushed over how happy she was to be in her new home. Charles, Tom, and Donny discussed what additional supplies they would need to bring in from Wickliffe to make repairs on the house. For dessert, Ethel brought out when she called her "award-winning brownies," complete with chocolate icing and homemade vanilla bean ice cream.

After dinner, Charles and the men unloaded mattresses while Paula, Ethel, and I washed dishes and then put the sheets and blankets on the beds as they were brought in.

Ethel went around the room, hugging everybody before she left. It was funny how she was the polar opposite of her husband,

Sam. Donny and Tom left to drive back to Wickliffe. It was 8:45 in the evening.

"Are we still having a 'prayer date'?" Charles whispered to me.

"We're praying, but it is not a date," I reminded him.

"Can't blame a guy for trying."

"Let's take a walk and find a good place," I suggested.

"I'm all yours," Charles grinned, but his smile faded at my stern look.

Paula was busy getting her children ready for bed, so Charles and I walked down the dirt road. I had no idea where we were headed, but I could hear the sound of my heart beating loudly in my ears. I hoped there was no way he could notice that or the fact that I was trying so very hard not to like him.

Chapter 18

The lightning bugs were flashing their lights around us, and the crickets were chirping as we made our way down the road. It quickly evolved into a simple path. Soon we could hear the murmur of a stream as the path took a sudden drop. As we stepped downward, Charles made sure he went first so that he would be the one to fall, should there be an unforeseen branch in the way.

In the blink of an eye, I stubbed my toe on a rock and fell toward Charles. He turned around quickly and caught me in his arms. The early September wind ruffled his hair. It was too dark to see the expression in his eyes, but his face was close to mine. I could smell the woodsy scent of his cologne.

"Katie..." he whispered.

I pushed myself away from him.

"I'm sorry...I'm clumsy, stumbling over that rock."

"I'm not sorry. I wish you'd do it again."

"Why? So you can laugh at me?"

"No, silly. So I'd have an excuse to hold you in my arms."

My face turned red. I could feel my cheeks burning, but I hoped it was too dark for him to see me.

"You know I'm here for another reason."

"Yes. To help save my soul because I'm such a rotten person to begin with." He turned away. "Maybe I don't want to be saved."

"But God heard you that night when you were going to kill yourself. You asked for help—right before God sent me to you."

"That's strange. I felt like I was so alone there that night."

"Don't you know you're never really alone? God is always with you."

There was a group of trees surrounding a stream. Charles lifted me down the last several feet of the embankment. Then we sat under the trees. On a whim, I threw off my shoes and dangled my feet in the water. It felt cool as it rushed against my skin.

Charles leaned back and stretched out his legs, close to the water. "Is this where we are going to pray?" he asked.

"I think so. It is a beautiful, peaceful setting for it. We even have God's symphony playing in the background."

"God's symphony?"

"It's what my family called the sound of water in nature. It's more beautiful than anything even Chopin, Mozart, or Beethoven could have written."

We listened in silence to the sound of rushing water for a few minutes.

"I see what you mean. I never thought of it that way, but it is beautiful."

The water swept against the rocks as we sat there, listening again.

"Let's think of several people we want to pray for," I said, breaking the silence. "Definitely, Sam."

"Yeah, what a jerk. He really needs some prayers."

"You would too if your son was fighting in the Vietnam War," I reminded him sternly.

"Well, you're actually right about that," Charles admitted. "Okay, who else?"

"Paula, Jessica, and Aaron...Plus, we need to pray for Paula's alcoholic ex-boyfriend."

"Him? He doesn't deserve our prayers! He nearly strangled me to death!"

"We need to pray for him that he changes his ways before it's too late."

"Don't you think you are being a little too virtuous? I really don't feel like praying for the guy."

"Prayer helps us even more than the people we're praying for."

"How? I'm still going to hate him."

"Do you think that drunk knows or cares that you hate him?"

"No. Of course not."

"So that hatred and anger hurt only you. Prayer takes the edge off that anger, and the more you pray for him, the less you hate him. Eventually, that hatred fades into nothing, and love takes its place and grows."

"You mean I need to keep on praying for him?" He sounded more than a little disgusted with the idea.

"It wouldn't hurt. It would help you, and it might even help him."

"I'll try it this once, but I can't make promises about the future."

"That's all I ask," I said with a smile. I couldn't expect him to instantly transform into a born-again Christian. Of course, that would have made my job easier.

"What do I do?" he asked, a little helplessly.

"Just close your eyes and listen." I closed my eyes to shut out the distractions. "God, thank you for this day You've given us to live in. Thank you for the health and food You've provided for us. Tonight, we want to pray for several people, asking You to bless and help them. Please bless Paula and her children as they begin their new lives here. Help them to be happy and grow in their love for You. Please help Paula's ex-boyfriend to get help before it is too late and teach him how to be a better man. Thank you for Ethel and the meal she brought us tonight. Please help Sam as he is struggling with his son being sent to fight in Vietnam. We ask that You keep his son safe while he is fighting for our country. Also, please watch over Charles and me as we go along on this adventure. Forgive us of our sins, as we have forgiven those who have sinned against us. Thank you for giving us Your Son, who died for us. In Jesus' name, Amen."

I opened my eyes. Charles was keenly studying my face in the darkness.

"So, do you think God heard all of that?"

"I know He did, or I wouldn't do it. It wouldn't make sense to pray if there was no God."

"How do you know there is one?"

"You can read the Bible, pray, and develop a relationship with Him. However, at some point, you just have to believe."

"Is there any scientific proof that the Bible and God are real?"

"There's all kinds of proof! The Dead Sea Scrolls have been found. There is scientific evidence the flood took place. There have been archaeological findings to support the Bible. But even after all of that, at some point, your faith has to kick in. You believe because of your love for God. He gave His only Son for us on the cross so that we could be forgiven of our sins. So, you confess that Jesus is the Son of God, and then you are baptized. You live a Christian life and teach others about Jesus so that they can be saved too. Throughout our lives, we work for God to strengthen our faith in Him. However, we can never earn our way to heaven. Because Jesus died for us on the cross, God gives us a home in heaven through His mercy and grace."

"If you were a Christian when you were alive, why did God send you back? Shouldn't you be in paradise with your family?"

"I am ashamed to admit it, but this is the first time I actually told someone about Jesus. I never told anyone when I was alive. I was always too busy—studying, dating, and shopping. I was just a bench warmer in church—nothing more. Everything else in my life seemed more important. Now that I'm dead, I know that only one thing really mattered: God and my relationship with Him."

"If what you're saying is true, then I really need to change my life. I don't even know much about Jesus. I just assumed that this life was it and that when you die, there's nothing afterward."

"But isn't this better? That once we die, we get new bodies and have eternal life?"

"Only if we go to heaven when we die. Going to hell for all eternity is worse than death. You only go through death once, but hell is forever."

"Why don't we read the Bible and get to know Jesus together?" I suggested. "I don't know as much about Him as I should. And this really is my last chance."

"It could be my last chance too. Those mobsters could catch up with me at any time and shoot me."

"Not on my watch." I tossed my hair back defiantly.

"And why do you care? Am I just your project?"

"You're my friend."

"If that's all we can ever be, then I'll take it. And so far, you've been a very good friend." He clasped my hand in his. His hand was warm and strong.

A silent, forbidden wish rose inside of me at that moment. I wished that things could be different, that I was fully human again. Because if I were alive and everything was normal, I knew I'd want to be much more than friends with Charles. We sat together like that, my hand in his, by the water in the cool darkness for quite a while. I tried to engrave that memory into my mind so that wherever I went, I could hold it in my heart forever.

Chapter 19

The next few days and weeks were very busy as we fixed up the house. Jessica and Aaron even helped as we scrubbed and cleaned the old place. We repainted every room. A couple of handymen from Wickcliffe helped us remodel the kitchen.

To save money, Charles wanted to repair the roof by patching it up himself. I insisted on going up there with him. He wasn't going to fall off and get killed while I was around.

It was now the middle of September. The leaves were starting to change colors. There was a cool breeze, and the hazy golden glow was in the sky that only happens in the fall. Charles headed up the ladder. I went up after him. It was a steep climb, as it was a two-story house.

"Can't you just stay on the ground?" he growled as he climbed. "Now, not only do I have to fix the roof; I have to worry about you falling off of it!"

"I resent that!" My eyes narrowed at him. "You're forgetting about my superhuman power. I could probably fly if I tried."

"Yeah, you'll fly off the roof and bust your head when you hit the ground," he snickered.

"How funny." I rolled my eyes.

We kept on climbing until we were on top of the roof. I must admit Charles looked incredible today. His dark, wavy hair glistened in the sun, and his silvery-blue eyes sparkled. His skin was tan from weeks of working in the sun. He had on a white T-shirt and jeans. A brown canvas tool belt was tied around his waist. He had never looked more manly. He pulled out his hammer and started to nail extra shingles to the roof to repair it. I had a bag of shingles slung over my back, so each time he needed a new one, I'd hand one to him.

The sun was hot up here, even though it was a cool day. I'd be glad when this job was over, although I was enjoying watching him work. He was completely absorbed in his work and didn't seem to mind or care that I was just sitting there watching him.

After he patched up the gaping holes and then reshingled them, we started carefully scooting back down toward the ladder.

"Why don't you hold my hand?" he offered. "I don't want you falling."

"What an insult!" I frowned. "I don't need to hold your hand! I'm the one who came up here to protect you!"

"Take heed, lest you fall," Gabriel's voice warned in my ear.

I stood up, and suddenly I lost my balance. I fell back and started sliding and then rolling off the roof.

"Katie!" Charles shouted. He jumped down, trying to catch me, risking his life just to save me. Even as I fell, I felt like a bumbling idiot. I crashed over the edge of the roof. For a second, I saw my life flash before my very eyes and wondered if it was possible to die a second time. My body flipped over. My hands scraped against something, and I blindly reached out and held on. Turns out, I was hanging onto the rain gutter, with my legs dangling precariously in midair.

"Hold on, Katie! I'm coming!" Charles rushed over and bent low. His hands now held mine.

"But you might fall trying to save me," I panted between breaths of air.

"What a great way to die," he grinned. He leaned back and pulled with his body weight until I was over the edge and could crawl onto the roof again.

Gabriel—what happened to my superhuman power? People with these powers don't fall off roofs, I thought.

"Pride goes before a fall," Gabriel told me quietly. "When you don't think you need God or anyone else, you fail."

"But you let me fall and almost die again," I protested out loud. "That's harsh."

"You are here to learn. Things won't always go the way you expect them to," Gabriel told me.

"How does falling off the roof teach me anything?"

"It teaches you that you still need the help of others," he said.

"Who are you talking to?" Charles asked with a puzzled expression. I kept forgetting no one but me could hear Gabriel's voice.

"You don't want to know," I warned him.

"It looked like you were having an intense conversation...with no one but yourself," Charles observed.

"Well, I do find myself a fascinating person to talk to," I joked.

"That's funny, so do I." Charles cast a sardonic grin my way.

I noticed a dimple in his right cheek when he smiled, and I felt my heart melting.

"Thanks for saving me from falling off the roof."

"It was fun."

We laughed. Then we sat on the roof and talked awhile.

At last, I wanted to mention something I'd had on my mind for quite some time.

"Could I ask a favor?"

"Anything," he answered.

"I'd like you to ask Paula out on a date."

"What? Why?" He was totally caught off guard.

"Because she needs you. Her kids need you..."

"But I don't feel that way about her."

"But you could—if you spent time with her and gave her a chance..."

"Is that what you really want?" His face was dark, almost as if he was mad at me.

"Yes," I said meekly.

"Then I'll do it." He turned away abruptly. "We'd better go on down." He started back down the ladder and motioned for me to follow. "I'll go first, though, so I can break your fall if I need to."

When we got back down, I noticed that there was an awkward silence between the two of us. You'd have thought I had asked him to jump off a cliff. Paula was a pretty woman, and I thought they'd make a cute couple.

Charles stomped off, and I decided to find another chore to keep me busy. I was hanging up freshly washed laundry on the line when Aaron tugged at my shirttail.

"Katie, why don't you stay with us forever? You and Charles could live with us. We could all be a family." He had blonde hair and big soulful blue eyes, a really beautiful kid. I had to let him down very gently.

I sat on a big tree stump in the backyard and pulled him onto my lap, and put my arms around him.

"I may not be able to stay here forever, but Charles might," I said softly. I would miss the children, Paula, and especially Charles, but this wasn't my life. Mine was already over, dead and gone.

"Why can't you stay? I love you."

"Let's just have fun while I'm here and not think about when I leave. I can promise you though, I'll never forget you."

"I'll never forget you either, Katie. You helped make our new home beautiful."

Suddenly Paula came running out of the house. Her eyes were shining, and she was breathless as she came up to me.

"Aaron, go play," she ordered her son. He slid off my lap and ran off in another direction. "Guess what, Katie! Charles asked me out for tonight! I'm so excited!"

"That's great." I wish I could've sounded happier, but for some reason, I wasn't. And I was the one who made him ask her out.

"Will you help me get all dolled up for our date?"

"Of course, I will." My voice was flat. I felt like kicking myself for acting so stupidly. I had no right to be anything other than excited for her.

"I am surprised he asked me out. I know you said you were just friends, but I still kinda thought you two were an item."

"Of course not!" I was almost too quick to shoot down her theory. "Charles and I could never be anything more than friends. I *want* him to date and see other women." That was the truth, as far as I was concerned.

"Then you don't mind?"

"Why would I mind? It's not like we were dating."

"All right. I won't worry then."

Hours later, I was fixing Paula's hair. I left her long auburn locks hanging straight and free about her shoulders, as was the style of the 1960s. I gave her pale pink lips and silvery-grey eyeshadow to bring out her blue eyes.

When I was through, she turned around to look in the mirror.

"Wow! I haven't looked this good since before I had kids!"

"I'm glad you like it." I gave her what turned out to be a stony smile in the mirror.

She had borrowed my long blue dress with bell sleeves and wore a silver peace sign necklace with it. I hated to admit it, but she would have looked cute, even if I hadn't helped her.

Charles was waiting at the door as Paula came down the stairs. I was right behind her.

"You look beautiful," Charles said.

Maybe I was imagining it, but it seemed like he was staring at me when he said that.

He had a bouquet of wildflowers in his hand that he gave to Paula when she got to the main floor.

"Thank you. You didn't have to do that," Paula told him.

"Oh yes, I did." Then he glared at me.

"You two have a great time together!" I said cheerfully.

"Don't worry. We will," Charles tossed the words over his shoulder nonchalantly, as he put his hand on the small of Paula's back and walked out with her like that.

I cringed. Then, I felt like slapping myself. I wanted Charles and Paula to be happy. After all, I was the one who had set them up. But somehow, I had just messed up everything, and I only had myself to blame.

Chapter 20

That night I read books to Aaron and Jessica. We played hide and seek, and I told them stories at bedtime: Cinderella, Sleeping Beauty, and Goldilocks and the Three Bears. These were the kind of stories my mother had told me when I was little. I tucked them in and gave them a hug.

"Don't leave me yet." Three-year-old Jessica patted the space beside her. "Stay."

"All right. Just for a little while." I laid down next to her. She was asleep in a few minutes, the sound of her relaxed breathing in my ears. Aaron was already snoozing away too. I stretched out and relaxed. Before I knew it, I was out of it too.

Hours later, I heard the door downstairs open, and then I heard light footsteps coming up the stairs. A ray of light crept into the room as Paula cracked the door open to check on her children.

I started to get up groggily.

"Did you have a good time?" I asked. Why was I even asking? Of course, they did.

"It was all right," Paula answered evenly.

My back shot up as I bounced into sitting position.

"What do you mean it was all right? You were so happy you were almost giddy earlier tonight!"

"I was never the woman he was interested in." There was a definite sadness in her voice.

"What do you mean?"

"Don't you know? It's you he wants, not me."

"Why would you say that?"

"He wouldn't shut up about you the whole evening. Katie did this; she said that. You might as well have come with us tonight."

"I am so sorry."

She gave me a little wave of her hand and shook her head.

"I'll be just fine. It's not like I was in love with him yet...but you are."

"What? Me? No way."

"What would be wrong with you falling for him? He's gorgeous, exciting, good-natured...If I can't have him, I wouldn't mind it so much if you got him."

"I appreciate you giving me the green light with Charles, but for reasons I can't get into, we can never be together."

"What a shame. You really are perfect together," Paula commented innocently.

"Yeah, I know." I couldn't deny it any longer. I squeezed her hand. "But don't ever tell him you think so."

"Honey, he probably already knows. What are you fighting it for?"

"I can't tell you. So, let's just agree not to talk about it again."

"All right. If that's what you want."

I got up and went quietly to my bedroom. I felt a lump in my throat, but I refused to cry. Paula had to be wrong. I didn't love him. I couldn't.

I was up half the night, so naturally, I woke up late, around 10:30 in the morning. I went downstairs. Everything was unusually quiet. I looked out the window and saw Paula playing with Aaron and Jessica. Charles was nowhere in sight. I rushed outside. I had a sinking feeling in my heart.

"Good morning, Paula! Have you seen Charles today?" I tried to keep the panic out of my voice.

Paula gazed at me with an almost guilty look.

"He's gone, Katie," she said simply.

"Gone? What do you mean gone?"

"He left this morning. He said to tell you goodbye for him and that he wishes you the best."

"I've got to find him."

"How are you going to find him?"

"I have my ways," I replied. I turned around. I was fuming. Who runs away from his guardian angel? He does, apparently—what a jerk. After all we'd been through together, and he sneaks off. I ran inside to be alone with my thoughts and closed my eyes to concentrate.

Gabriel, where did I go wrong? I asked him silently.

"You let your feelings get in the way," his voice echoed in my ear. I jumped. I hadn't expected an answer so soon.

"It's the human part of me," I protested out loud. "Why couldn't you make the person I was going to help ugly, fat, and bald?"

"Do you want a new assignment?" Gabriel offered.

"Not really."

"Then stop complaining."

"Could you please help me find him?"

"If I do, you'd better agree to act more heavenly than humanly."

"I will. I'll be on my best behavior." The truth was that I couldn't imagine not ever seeing Charles again. But I had to repress this weird crush I had on him. My human days were over. But if I could just help him and complete my mission, everything would be all right.

"I'll help you find him..."

"Oh, thank you!" I blurted out.

"...but this time," he continued, "you might not get a miracle every time you mess up."

"Okay. I'll try to do better this time," I promised.

"Good. Because you must."

I opened my eyes. I was sitting in the front seat of Charles' Mustang.

"So, why did you run off?" I asked.

He looked over and saw me there beside him. His face registered total shock. He was staring so intently; he didn't notice as his car wandered into the next lane.

A loud horn blared from an eighteen-wheeler. I screamed as a flashback of how I died was unfolding before my very eyes. Charles swerved back onto our side of the road just in time.

"What in the world are you doing here? Did you sneak like a stowaway in the backseat of the car?"

"How could I have done that when I was asleep while you left? We both know that would have been impossible."

"But it is also impossible for you to suddenly magically appear in my car. Did you drug me? LSD? Marijuana, perhaps?"

"Where would I even get drugs around here? The town square at Wickliffe?"

In spite of himself, he let out a laugh.

"You're right. That's not going to happen."

"They—" I glanced up meaningfully, "—sent me back to you. So don't run away next time. You're stuck with me—for a while."

"The 'for a while' is the part that bothers me. Why can't you just stay forever?"

"Because I'm not human anymore."

"You seem human enough to me." He caressed my hair lightly with his hand.

I scooted over toward my window.

"I can't stay if you do stuff like that."

"I don't know how to just be your friend."

"Well, you better learn fast. I only have a limited time to help you. After that, you may not even remember me."

"I could never forget you."

"That choice may not be up to you."

"They'd take even my memories of you?"

"We have to be prepared, just in case."

"Then before I forget, I want to tell you—"

"Please don't."

He shook his head. He was so stubborn.

"I'm falling in love with you. That's why I was so angry at you, trying to set me up with Paula. Paula's a nice lady, but she isn't you. I left this morning because I was sure you didn't feel the same way since you were trying to push Paula on me."

I turned my head away, looking anywhere but into his eyes.

"I may feel the same way, but there's nothing we can do about it. Are you sure you couldn't develop feelings for her? You'd be a great father to her children."

"Maybe in another world I could love Paula. If I hadn't met you first."

"I promise I won't try to hook you up with her again. If you go back with me, we could finish working on her house and make sure she has a good church where she can go. She needs a close church family to help her raise those kids."

"And what do we do about us?"

Boy, he was persistent.

"There is no us. Nor will there ever be. But no one says we can't be best friends."

He grinned. "I'll take it."

"All this drama has made me really hungry. Why don't you turn the car around, and we'll find a good hamburger joint on the way back? I could really use a juicy cheeseburger about right now."

He made a big U-turn on the highway. Luckily, there were no eighteen-wheelers this time. We headed back toward Lovelaceville. I had a lot of work to do with him. But for now, at least we were headed in the right direction.

Chapter 21

By late afternoon, we were back in Lovelaceville. We turned into the dirt driveway of Paula's home. She and the kids happened to be sitting on the front porch. When she saw us, she jumped off the porch and ran up to us. Aaron and Jessica were right behind her.

"Where have you been? I thought you might never come back!" she said, her eyes wide.

"We can't leave you yet!" I got out of the car, and Aaron and Jessica jumped into my arms. It made me wish I had lived long enough to experience having kids of my own.

"Come inside! I'm frying up some chicken and okra. I'm also cooking macaroni and cheese and mashed potatoes for dinner!"

And just like that, we were a part of their family again. It felt good to belong somewhere.

That night, we had an incredible dinner of southern fare. No one made food like they did in the South. Paula was a great cook.

"Why don't you two stay here with us indefinitely? This house is huge...You and Charles could get married..." Paula looked at us hopefully across the table.

I kicked her under the table.

"Paula, I don't know how you came up with such an idea," I laughed nervously. "Why you just went out with him last night."

"Yes, and we all know how well that worked out," she said ruefully. "It's just I saw your face when I told you Charles left. You looked like you had been hit by an eighteen-wheeler."

I kicked her again. She obviously didn't get the message the first time.

"Ow!" she yelped. "That's going to leave a bruise."

I glared at her. If looks could kill, I'd be doing CPR on her dead corpse right now. Charles coughed loudly, clearly trying to cover up a chuckle.

"Well, I'm still glad you came back, for whatever reason," she said as an awkward silence filled the air. Even the kids were silently staring at us like we were crazy. "Katie, would you like to help me wash the dishes?"

I felt like taking the dishes and breaking them over her head. Instead, I smiled sweetly and said, "Of course."

Charles and the kids went to play outside, which left Paula staring at me nervously.

"Wanna chat?" I said between clenched teeth.

"Uh, I guess. Well, not really."

"Don't worry. You can say embarrassing things out loud now. No one is around to hear, so I won't kick you. Right now."

"Okay then...What is up with you and Charles? He obviously likes you, and you like him. What would be so terrible about the two of you getting together?"

"We are friends only, Paula. I'm sorry your date went badly, but that doesn't mean Charles and I are getting together. Actually, we both came back to help you and the kids out a little longer."

"The kids and I will be fine." Her neck stiffened a bit. "We are not some charity project that you need to take care of."

"I didn't mean it that way. We care about you, and we want to do everything we can to help you get started in your new life."

"I am grateful for all you both have done for us. But don't you have somewhere else you need to be? Don't you have a family...or a job?"

"Doing good is my job right now. And I can't tell you where I'm from or who my family is. You wouldn't know them. But while I'm here, I want to make sure you're on the right path. Do you know Jesus?"

"What?" She was startled. "Are you one of those Jesus-lovers?"

"I'm proud to say that I am."

"I wondered where He was all those times Claude beat me up. I prayed night after night for someone to come and save me."

"Maybe He sent us."

"Well, He sure took His sweet time."

"His timetable is not like ours. One thousand years can be like a day to Him."

"Why did He even let me meet that drunk bum?"

"God doesn't promise to take away all the bad experiences in our lives. He just promises to be there with us as we go through them."

"I could have sworn I was alone every time he beat me up."

"You're never alone. God knows even when a sparrow dies. And you are much more valuable to Him than a bird."

"I was baptized when I was a teenager, but I fell away. I had a husband I loved more than life itself. Then God took him away. I got lost. That was when I met Claude and wasted years with him. We weren't married. We were living in sin. What would Jesus think of that?"

"He wouldn't condemn you. And neither do I. He would want you to learn from your mistakes, repent, and get on the right path."

"How do I start?"

"Let's have a Bible study together tonight. And right now, we could pray."

"I don't know if I even remember how."

"Listen to me while we pray. Think about the words and say them with me in your heart. Remember to say, 'In Jesus' name' at the end. It's like putting the postage stamp on an envelope. That ensures that Jesus takes our prayers to God."

"Can we pray now?"

"We can pray anytime and any place. That's the great thing about prayer: God is always ready to listen to us, no matter where we are or what we are doing." We shut our eyes and clasped our hands together.

"God, we praise Your holy name. Thank you for giving Paula and her children a new life here. Please forgive Paula for her past sins and mistakes. Take away her guilt and replace it with Your grace. Please help her to know that all have sinned and fallen short of Your glory.

Help her to turn away from her past and toward Your love, so it can fill her heart and soul. Please help her as she raises her children and guides them toward You. Come into her heart and fill it with Your goodness. In Jesus' name, Amen." I opened my eyes. Paula was smiling and had a beautiful glow about her. "How do you feel?"

"I haven't felt this good in years. I feel like a new person!" Her face said it all.

It was only then that I could begin to comprehend the full majesty of God and the miracles that only He could manifest in our lives. And Paula was one of those miracles.

Chapter 22

That night, we studied the Bible and went over 1 Corinthians 13, the chapter of love. I thought it was a good place to start. Paula was a quick learner. Over the next few days, we studied the life of Jesus and had Bible classes with Jessica and Aaron too. Even Charles attended and seemed to enjoy it.

Paula and I drove around Wickliffe until we found her a good Bible-based church that she and her children could attend. We also got Paula a job as a waitress at a local meat-and-three restaurant in Wickliffe. Charles found her an inexpensive used car so she could drive there to work every day.

Things were going so well. Any day now, I expected Gabriel would call me up to those pearly gates. I felt ready to go. Paula and the kids were doing great. Even Charles was happy. He spent his days renovating and repairing the house and his nights reading and studying the Bible with us. Each Sunday morning, evening, and Wednesday night, Charles would drive us to church services. The people there were quaint country folks with warm hearts and deep faith. I wish we could have stayed with them and Paula and the kids forever.

I didn't know how I could have been much happier or more at peace, but God had even more miracles in store for Paula that would deepen my faith.

We were in a church service, and our minister was preaching on how God could forgive us, no matter what we've done. It was about starting over as a spiritual newborn in the loving arms of God.

Paula obviously identified with the starting over part. Her eyes were filled with tears.

"I'm going to get baptized again," she whispered to me as she squeezed my hand.

"Really? But you were baptized once before." I was a little puzzled.

"Well, this time, it's going to take," she grinned. Then, she suddenly looked nervous and vulnerable. "Could you go up there with me?"

"I'd be happy to," I said without hesitation. I was a little nervous inside about walking up there in front of a room full of people. Then I reminded myself of Paula's courage, re-committing to the Lord and starting a new spiritual journey. Besides, why should I mind being in front of these people? I was already dead. Chances were, I wouldn't even be around them much longer.

At the end of the sermon, the preacher offered the invitation.

"Are there any of you who would like to accept Jesus Christ as your Lord and Savior? Then you can be baptized into a new way of life as a Christian. If you need our prayers, please come forward now as we sing."

Paula and I stood up and walked toward the front of the building. My cheeks burned, but I kept on walking. Her hand trembled in mine, and I knew she was scared too. We sat down on the front pew.

The preacher had the warmest smile imaginable on his face. Somehow, I could see the light of God shining in his kind brown eyes. I wasn't scared anymore.

"Are you both wanting to be baptized today? Or do you need our prayers?" he whispered eagerly.

"My name is Paula, and I have come forward to be rebaptized. I was baptized years ago, but I fell away. Now, I would like to recommit myself to the Lord. My friend, Katie, came up here with me so I wouldn't be alone."

"Kate, do you need to be baptized, or can we pray for you?"

"Well...I've been baptized, but could you pray for me?" I may have been dead, but I was alive enough to know I still needed prayers.

"Of course, we can pray for you. What struggles are you having?" The preacher's voice was soothing and soft, yet he also came across as keenly intelligent and direct.

"I just need the prayers of the Church to help me make the best decisions and to do the right things. I'm going through a challenging time, and I was going to ask the congregation to pray to the Lord to help me through it."

"Of course, we will. I'm so glad you came." The preacher squeezed my hand warmly.

Strangely, I was glad I did too. I had never done anything like this when I was alive, but if I had, maybe I would be with my family now in paradise instead of ending up somewhere in-between. I should have cared more about my spiritual destiny. Now, I could see that was the only thing that truly mattered about my former life. With the prayers of the congregation, maybe I could get it right this time.

The preacher then turned to Paula, and they huddled together in whispers for several minutes. Then the preacher stood up.

"I have two ladies here who have both responded. Katie is going through a difficult time and would like us to pray for her, that she'll make the right decisions and that God will be her guide now." He led a beautiful prayer for me. Then he turned to Paula. "And Paula has come forward to be baptized. She wants to recommit her life to the Lord. Paula, I am going to ask you the most important question you'll ever answer. Do you believe that Jesus Christ is the Son of God?"

"I do," Paula answered.

"Thank you for your confession, Paula. I know the angels in heaven are rejoicing this very moment." The church was small, and they had no baptistery there, but when weather permitted, they had baptisms in a nearby creek. In the winter, they drove to a larger church that had a baptistery, but it was fifteen miles away. We formed a line of cars with the preacher's car leading the way. He led us all to a creek that was in the midst of several clusters of trees. The water was about four feet deep in the middle. The sun sparkled like diamonds on the water—such a picturesque setting for a baptism.

Charles and I stood together holding hands with Jessica and Aaron. The congregation also gathered there.

Paula had never looked so pretty. Her face was literally glowing. She and the preacher waded into the water as he held her arm. She was in a white, flowing gown that she borrowed from the church to use for the baptism. She looked like an angel, her long thick, auburn hair hanging loosely down her back.

"Paula, I baptize you in the name of the Lord, Jesus Christ, and the Holy Spirit for the remission of your sins," the preacher announced.

He lowered her until she was completely covered by the water and then brought her back up.

I was so happy. God used me to help bring one of His lost sheep back into the fold.

We all sang "Shall We Gather at the River," which was perfect for the location. Then we sang "Paradise Valley." As Paula and the preacher walked back to the bank, the congregation gathered around her and hugged and congratulated her. I was one of them. Her kids were wearing big smiles. Even Charles had been paying rapt attention to this whole process and offered a congratulatory handshake to Paula as she stood, surrounded by the people of the church.

It was one of those perfect, magical moments that you remember for the rest of your life. Perfect. Until...

I turned around. I had felt someone watching us several yards away. Standing in the midst of the crowd, I saw them. The two goons were back! The taller one nodded at me in recognition as a knowing smile curled his lips. The shorter one's eyes narrowed as he spotted Charles, and his hand automatically shifted as it reached for the gun he kept in his pocket.

I elbowed Charles. He looked at me immediately. I motioned my head toward the two thugs.

I pushed through the crowd that was gathered around Paula. First, I hugged her again for her decision to start a new spiritual journey with Christ. But then I quickly pulled her aside.

"Paula...Charles and I have to get out of here, fast."

Her eyes registered shock.

"Why? Are you in danger?"

"Not me." I was practically dead already, but I couldn't tell her that. "It's Charles. These two men are after him. If we stay any longer, you and your children could be in danger," I warned her.

Tears sprang to Paula's eyes. "Do you have to go? In a weird way, I felt like we were becoming a family. You did everything for me. I have this new life because of you, even my being re-baptized today. You took an interest in me and actually changed the way I thought."

"I didn't change you. God did."

"Well, you helped. I thank God for sending you to me."

"I'm glad He used me to bring you back to Him. Now, you must continue moving forward on your own, and I know you can do it!"

"So, I'll never see you or Charles again?" Then she added shyly, "You're the closest I've ever had to a sister."

"At this point, I have no idea what will happen in the future. I do hope we get to meet again, if not on earth, then in heaven. You'll always be my sister too." I hugged her once more.

"Can I have a hug too?" Charles had walked up behind us.

"Always," Paula replied.

"I'm proud of all you've accomplished," Charles told her.

"I couldn't have done it without you both." Paula called Jessica and Aaron to her and told them we were leaving. They threw their arms around us and clung to us, not wanting us to leave.

"We'll try to come back and see you if we can," I told them as I started to gently untangle myself from the arms of the children. I knew that there was a big chance I might never see them again in this life. Maybe that was why I hung on to them just a moment longer.

"Hurry, Katie," Charles said below his breath. The thugs were standing just a few feet away, watching our every move.

"I'm coming." I turned back to Paula. "Goodbye, and God bless you and your children always."

Paula had tears in her eyes as she nodded silently and waved goodbye.

Charles and I quickly slipped through the crowd, putting just a little more distance between us and the hitmen. I looked back at them. While watching us trying to get away, they were both grinning smugly, as if they knew that there was no hope for us. I wondered if they were right.

Chapter 23

Charles and I hopped into his Mustang and roared off. I watched as the two men slowly walked to their car and got in. They were like two cats playing with their prey, so sure of themselves.

"We can't go back to the house for anything, or they'll know where Paula and the kids live."

"I know." In my mind, I said a silent goodbye to my 1960s wardrobe. Easy come, easy go. At least Paula would have some beautiful clothes to wear.

Charles was barreling down those old Kentucky country back roads like a madman. I just hoped that no kids were playing out in the streets. I glanced behind me. The gunmen were in a black Cadillac not too far behind us. I watched in horror as the bigger of the henchmen stuck his head out the passenger side with a pistol in his hand.

"Charles, they're going to shoot at us. We don't have a gun! What are we going to do?"

"Well, you don't have to worry since you're already dead. Me, however, that's a different story. But don't worry that beautiful head of yours. I've got a plan."

He stepped on the gas. Our Mustang started to edge ahead from the Cadillac. That was a good thing too. I heard the blast of their gun, and a bullet whizzed by a few inches from my window. Charles responded by pushing the car even faster. His chiseled jaw was clenched, and his knuckles were white around the wheel. Soon, we were far enough away so that their Cadillac looked like a toy. We turned around a curve and were out of sight. Suddenly Charles swerved down a dirt road.

"Where are we going?" Curiosity had gotten the best of me.

"I have no idea. So maybe they won't either. That's the game plan."

He made several other sharp turns until we were literally in the middle of nowhere. He saw a huge barn with gigantic double doors that were wide open. He drove us on a gravel road and then through an open pasture to get to it. We passed some huge cows behind a fence nearby who looked up at us in surprise.

He drove us into the barn, jumped out of the car, and closed the doors. It was dark except for a few patches missing from the roof where we could see the blue sky. The barn had the smell of damp earth, piles of fresh hay, and farm animals. I knew the longer I was there, the more I'd get used to the smell. I hoped so, anyway.

"How long do we get to stay in these lovely accommodations?" I asked. I had always been a city girl.

"We should probably spend several hours here. I want them to wear themselves out trying to look for us. Then maybe they'll turn around or stop somewhere for a while to rest. We can sleep now and then leave in the middle of the night."

"Uh, there aren't exactly beds here."

"I'll make a couple of places for us to rest." He began forming two oblong piles of hay, shaped like miniature beds.

"Aren't there bugs in that stuff?"

Charles gave me a wry grin.

"We'll be okay for a few hours."

"If you say so." I still wasn't sure about lying down on a bed of hay. At a time like this, I missed the 1,000 thread count Egyptian cotton sheets I had splurged on in my former life.

I gingerly knelt down into the hay and was happily surprised at how fresh it smelled. I was getting ready to lie down when Charles was suddenly at my side. I stood up again.

"Here, take my coat." He spread the coat over the hay.

"But...don't you need it?"

"I'll be all right," he grinned. Then his face turned serious. "I do want to thank you for staying with me."

"I don't exactly have a choice. You are my assignment."

"Even so, I wouldn't want to be going through this alone. I don't know what I'd do without you here with me." His face was close to mine.

"Really, it's nothing."

"It's everything...to me."

His arms slowly edged around my waist and pulled me closer to him. I didn't—and couldn't—resist him. It was as if I was in a foggy dream. The dark dampness of the barn surrounded me. Yet, I was warm in his arms. I could smell his masculine cologne. His lips were mere inches from mine. I could stop him if I wanted to. Problem was, I didn't want to.

My arms slid automatically around his neck as if we'd done this so many times before. I made a snap decision and pulled his head closer.

His lips touched mine, and it was like fourth of July fireworks. I had resisted him for so long, and I couldn't do it anymore. His lips felt soft and tender. We stood there for what may have been moments or hours. I lost all track of time, so I couldn't tell.

"Marry me," he whispered so softly, I almost couldn't hear him. I pushed us apart.

"Marry you? I can't marry you! I'm already dead!"

"You felt very alive to me just a moment ago," he grinned.

"That can't ever happen again!" I shook my head in disgust. What was I doing? I was so weak!

"Was it that terrible?" He winced, looking like I had slapped him.

"The kiss? No! It was great. Too great! It should never have happened. 'We' can never happen. That kiss was my leading you on when there is no future for us."

He reached out for me, but I stepped back.

"But you felt something. I know you did."

"What I felt is irrelevant. We can't be together. I'm already dead. Any moment now, they could call me back. And then, we'll never see each other again."

"Couldn't you ask them to change the rules?" He pulled me to him and gently stroked my hair. "I really can't help it if I've fallen in love with you."

If the barn hadn't been so dark, he could have seen the shock and dismay that clearly registered on my face. Shock because no man had ever told me he loved me. Dismay because of what could never be. I was also disgusted with myself. How could I have been so weak and human?

Suddenly, the barn seemed stifling and claustrophobic. I ran over the hay-strung floor and flung open the door.

"Wait!" Charles tried to warn me.

A volley of gunfire met me as I nearly ran outside. I immediately pushed the door shut again. The goons had been waiting to ambush us. They must have somehow seen where we had been headed and had followed us. Now, we were trapped in the barn!

"What are we going to do?"

"Look!" Charles grinned. There were some old rifles leaned up against the wall. Charles walked over and nonchalantly picked one up and examined it. "Loaded too!"

I thanked God for saving Charles' life once again.

"Come on!" Charles grabbed my hand. "I have a plan." He ran toward the loft. I had no choice but to follow.

He motioned for me to climb up the ladder first.

"Uh...that looks a little rickety..."

"Don't worry. I'll be right behind you. I'll break your fall." Something in his grin told me he'd enjoy doing so too.

I rolled my eyes and started climbing. Once we were both there, we had a good view of the two thugs from our vantage point. Charles pushed a bale of hay over in front of the window, so we would have cover. They were waiting, crouched beside their Cadillac, watching the door of the barn for any signs of life.

Charles cocked his rifle. I started to say something.

He squeezed my hand and whispered, "Shhh..."

He concentrated and carefully took aim. Then he quickly fired three shots. The first shot flattened the Cadillac's front right tire. The second shot blew the front tire out on the left side. Then he paused and aimed with precision. The rifle went off. I heard the big guy yelp in pain, clutching his shoulder.

"That'll buy us some time. Hurry, let's go!" he said quickly.

"Go where?" The last time I checked, we were still trapped in the barn.

"You'll see."

We were back down the ladder in no time. He snatched his coat from the ground and threw it in the backseat of the car.

"Get in." He opened the passenger door for me. Then he jumped in on the other side. He put the car in reverse as far as it would go until we were about two inches from the back barn wall. Then he slammed the gas pedal to the floor. We crashed through the barn doors.

I had no idea what would happen next.

Chapter 24

We barreled across the barnyard. The goons were in shock. Luckily, we had them off guard. The little man took some shots at us but missed every time as we roared past him. The big guy clutched his right arm in pain and frustration. He couldn't shoot us because Charles had intentionally injured his shooting arm on his right side. Instead, he clenched his left fist and glared at us as we passed by.

"They can't follow us with two flat tires," Charles told me. "They may have one spare tire, but there's no way they'll have two. They'll have to walk somewhere and get help, and they'd better hurry, so the big one doesn't bleed to death."

"You could have killed both of them. I'm glad you didn't. But how come you chose not to? And where did you learn to shoot like that?"

"I may be a lot of things, but I'm no murderer. Even those hired killers have mothers somewhere who love them. As for the shooting, I once dallied with the idea of becoming a policeman. I had some training with guns."

"Why didn't you become a policeman?"

"I hate violence."

I giggled. "And look at you now: plowing through barn doors in your convertible, shooting a mobster in his shoulder, flattening the tires of their getaway car with two blasts of your gun. That's impressive, I'll have to say."

He didn't laugh. "I didn't choose this, Katie. Just as you didn't choose to come down here and help me."

"I'm glad I've been here to help you through this—I mean it."

He smiled and stretched his arm across the back of the seat. I moved over till I was next to him and leaned my head on his shoulder. I knew I was sending him the wrong message in doing so, but I was too tired to care. Getting shot at was draining.

After several hours, we were driving through the Mark Twain

National Forest in Missouri. I only knew that because I glimpsed a sign as we sped by. There were masses of dark trees for miles, occasionally broken up by old farmhouses. It was kind of spooky at night. We were the only ones on the road. It would have been easy to pretend we were the last people alive on earth.

Suddenly, I spotted an old rambling hotel that looked right out of the movie *Psycho*. I wondered how it stayed in business. I elbowed Charles and motioned toward the hotel.

Charles almost drove right by it, but when he saw where I was pointing, he made a sharp U-turn, and we skidded into the parking lot.

"We'll park in the back just in case those two nut jobs are still searching for us."

"Good idea," I agreed.

Charles booked us two separate suites, for which I was grateful. I sure didn't want to be tempted to kiss him again.

Our rooms were small but surprisingly clean. My bedding was in olive green, and the walls were done in orange and yellow flower wallpaper—more lovely 60s décor.

I fell into a sound sleep, but in the middle of the night, I could feel someone was watching me. My eyes popped open.

There was Gabriel.

"What do you think you're doing?" His voice broke like thunder into my room.

"Uh...you mean the kiss, obviously..." How embarrassing. I hadn't planned on having to explain myself to an angel.

"Of course, I mean the kiss! You're breaking all the rules! You're close to being suspended from this case! You know what that means?"

"That I get another case?" That would almost be a relief. Maybe they could give me some wrinkled fat old geezer that would never in a million years make me swoon.

"No. It means that you will be explaining yourself to God as to why you failed to finish your mission."

"So, where would I go after that? You could put me back on earth as another human...You know, like reincarnation," I suggested.

"There is no such thing as reincarnation. Try hard not to be so dense. If you don't complete your mission, you don't get a third chance. That's why this is so serious."

"I understand. I'll do my best not to mess up again. I'm not sure what to do next. Those two gunmen are probably still on our trail. They could kill Charles!"

"Don't worry about what could hurt his body. You are only here to guard his soul and help save it."

"But I don't want him to die!"

"What a human thought! The death of the human body is not something to be afraid of if one is a Christian."

"Charles isn't a Christian yet, so if he dies now, he's not going to make it to heaven. I've got to keep him alive!"

"I don't know how long you will be able to keep him alive."

"What do you mean? He's going to die?" I couldn't even fathom a world without Charles in it.

"I only meant that I don't know what the future holds. I certainly can't guarantee a fairytale ending."

"I don't care about fairytale endings! I just want him to live!" I was fighting back tears. I hadn't known I cared about him this much.

"You care more than you should."

"I know. That has been my downfall. I need your help, Gabriel. I really don't know where to go from here."

"Keep on leading him to Christ. And prepare him for the life he must lead when you are gone. One thing you could do is reunite him with the family he lost years ago. His mother is gone, but his sister and father are still alive. Your next task is to find Charles' sister. We'll worry about his father later."

When Gabriel told me where Lydia, Charles' sister, was, I grimaced. It would be challenging to get her out of there, to say the least. And if I wasn't careful during this mission, I could lose Charles for good.

Chapter 25

I awoke late the next morning to Charles knocking on my door. When I opened it, he looked me up and down and blurted out, "Wow. You look rough."

"Not the reaction I wanted, Charles." I glared at him.

"Did you sleep well?"

Actually, I stayed up most of the night talking with an angel about you. So, if I look rough, it's your fault, I thought to myself. Of course, I couldn't tell him that, though. "Let's just say I had a few nightmares during the night."

"I wish I had known. I could have been there to comfort you."

"I don't need your comfort, Charles," I said through clenched teeth. The stress of the situation was really getting to me.

"Grouchy a bit?" he asked with that disarming smile of his.

I felt my knees melting.

"It's hard to stay grouchy when you're here," I replied before I could stop the words from tumbling out. Then I berated myself.

What was I doing, flirting with him like that? Gabriel had already given me my final warning.

"Could I invite you to lunch in a little while?"

"Yeah. I need a cheeseburger, fast!" Stress was making me mighty hungry.

For a beat-up old hotel, they had incredible food. A little old lady named Ida put a huge juicy cheeseburger in front of me, the size of a small child's head. I sat there staring at it for a few minutes like it was a piece of art.

"If you don't want that cheeseburger, I can eat it," Charles offered. He had ordered a grilled cheese sandwich, but what I had evidently looked so much bigger and better.

"Don't touch my cheeseburger if you know what is good for you," I threatened.

He suppressed a smile, not realizing how serious I was. I started to chew it slowly, enjoying the warm grease of the one-hundred percent beef patty and the delicious melted cheddar cheese. I was in another world. After I chowed down on a few bites, I was ready to get down to business.

"We've got to find your sister," I managed to say while enjoying one of the best cheeseburgers ever.

"My sister? What made you think of her? I haven't seen her for over twenty years. We were split up as children in the orphanage. I wouldn't even know what she looks like. They may have even changed her name. I've come to grips with the reality that I'll most likely never see her again."

"Well, forget that reality because you are going to see her again."

"How? I don't even know where to look for her."

"I do."

"How would you know?"

"They—" I nodded my head upward, "told me."

"Are you sure you're not on something?"

I rolled my eyes at him.

"I'm really going to get to see my sister again?"

I nodded. "She's just a few miles from here. The catch is that she's in a cult, and we've got to get her out."

"So, she's hidden deep in the Mark Twain Forest as a member of a cult?"

"Basically, yes."

"Wow. What are the chances? We just ended up in the middle of the Mark Twain Forest, and she's a few miles away?"

"There are no chances. God led us here so we could help her."

"I'm ready. Let's go find her."

"Hold your horses, buddy. Let's get a plan first." Gabriel had given me detailed directions as to where the cult was hidden in the forest. We were to drive down the highway about ten more miles, take several dirt roads, and then walk a few miles.

Charles and I planned and schemed for a while. Eventually, I felt like we were almost prepared, or at least as prepared as we could be, to infiltrate a cult full of crazy people and rescue one of their members.

That night we drove as far as the dirt roads would take us into the middle of the forest. Luckily, there was a full moon, but it was still eerie. The trees stood tall like dark silent strangers. The only sound was the occasional ghostly call of an owl.

We walked for what seemed like days down footpaths and sometimes straight through bushy forest. My dress was in tatters from catching on thorns and branches. I imagined Charles' clothes were a mess now too. I just couldn't see them clearly in the night.

When I caught the heavy, sweet smell of pot drifting through the woods, I knew we were close. There was also the sound of a faint chanting in some other language. As we got closer, the chanting was louder, and the smell of pot was overwhelming. We were probably getting high just from standing there.

We suddenly came into a clearing. There were about two dozen people sitting around a huge bonfire. They were dressed in long white robes with a brown rope tied around the waist. Some had their eyes closed as they slowly chanted. Those with their eyes open looked as if they were in a trance, staring with glassy eyes into the fire. They didn't even notice we were there, which was very creepy.

As if he had known we were coming, a tall, lithe man with long gray hair stepped out of one of several tents and studied our faces.

"Who are you, and why have you come?" His piercing gray eyes watched our every move.

"We've heard about you, sir. We have traveled far to meet you. We would like to become your followers." I said, making it up as I went along.

"What have you heard about us?" His bushy eyebrows arched with interest.

"That you know the answers we are searching for, and we can find peace and fulfillment by being your followers."

"You are willing to make me your master?"

Whatever floats your boat, I thought. These cult leaders were so arrogant. Out loud, I answered, "We are more than willing, sir."

"You will find your new attire in tent number two. After you are dressed, we will go over the rules of our clan and the process of your initiation." He pointed toward a tent, which was our cue to skedaddle. I was already worried about this 'initiation.' What were they going to do? Blow-torch our fingertips?

We ambled toward the tent. Inside, a woman with long straight brown locks and stony jade green eyes explained what we would need to do.

"Here is your new attire." She handed us each a long white robe with a rope belt. "You will discard your old garments by throwing them into the bonfire. This is a symbol of how you are throwing away your old life in order to have a new one."

"Uh, this is a designer tie. Couldn't I just keep that?" Charles protested.

I elbowed him.

"Everything must go." The woman looked at Charles sternly.

He nodded his head meekly, but when the woman turned around, he rolled his eyes at me. I snickered a little.

The woman's head snapped back at us. "If you aren't serious about joining us, then please leave. We only want followers who are passionate about serving our master."

What a drag this cult was. If I had been alive during this decade and was cult-obsessed, I definitely wouldn't have chosen this one.

Out loud, I replied, "It is an honor and privilege to serve our master. His fame has spread throughout the land." I didn't even know the guy. I was totally winging this, so I hoped she believed me.

She nodded in agreement. She had a glazed look in her eyes like the stoned campers outside.

"By the way, there are two tents on either side, the left one for men, the right one for women. You may go to your respective tents to change into your new attire."

We went to our tents. On the way, I saw the members again. This time they were singing some weird song in another language and swaying to the music as if they were drunk. They were in their own little world and didn't even notice me walking by.

I opened the tent, and the inside was illuminated with a lantern. There, in the corner, was a crumpled figure shaking with sobs. The white robe of her back was streaked with blood.

She heard me come in, and startled, quickly turned around. She crouched with graceful cat-like movements. Her hands were on the ground. She winced as though the sudden movement hurt her. She'd obviously been beaten.

"Don't hurt me," she whispered. Her bright silvery-blue eyes gazed up at me, wide with fear. Those eyes were Charles' eyes.

"I'm not going to hurt you," I whispered back. "What's your name?" I already knew.

"Lydia."

My heart skipped a beat. We had found her.

Chapter 26

"Who did this to you?" I had a vague idea: one of those nut jobs outside.

"Damion, the leader of this crazy place. He said I was chosen to pay for the sins of the cult. But that's not true! He's punishing me because I won't marry him! He said he wanted to make me his princess and that this would be our kingdom. But he's thirty-eight years older than me...He's tried to kiss me before, and he's just disgusting! Please, help me!" Then she started crying again.

I hugged her lightly, so I wouldn't hurt her.

"We'll help you," I whispered into her hair.

"But aren't you here to be a new member?" she asked.

"Yeah...don't think that's going to happen. By the way, would you like to get out of here?"

"Would I! But it may be too late. They'll find me. Damion said he would go to the ends of the earth to find me if I ever tried to get away."

"What a jerk. He doesn't have as much power over you as you think he does. How in the world did you get here?"

"I was homeless and hitchhiking through Missouri, looking for a job. The last driver I was riding with got drunk and tried to make a pass at me. When I turned him down, he opened his car door while he was still driving and threw me out. I landed in the Mark Twain National Forest, with no more than the clothes on my back.

"I had no food or shelter for four days until Damion found me half-frozen in the snow. He saved my life when he brought me to the camp. Eventually, though, he tried to get me addicted to drugs, but I refused.

"He had a certain fascination for me because he saw he couldn't control me. He wanted me to call him 'master' like his other followers did, but I wouldn't. Jesus is my only 'Master,' not this creep.

"Anyway, Damion announced to me three days ago that we were

going to be married. I replied, 'How dare you tell me that we are going to be married! The United States is still a free country, and I will marry whomever I choose. If you were the last person alive in the world, I still wouldn't choose you.' He isn't used to being told 'no.' He said I would be sorry for refusing him."

"So, he beat you?" I still couldn't believe a grown man could act like that, using brute force to punish someone because he didn't get his way.

"Oh, yeah," she touched her back ruefully. "I wasn't surprised; he's done it before. This time, he made a show of it, telling his followers I had to pay for their sins. That was his explanation for beating me with his leather whip. He whispered afterward that my punishment would be worse next time if I kept on refusing to marry him."

"You've got to get out of here before he kills you."

"How? He's watching me every minute. He's obsessed with me. I've tried running away several times, but each time, he hunts me down like an animal."

"Well, this time will be different..."

"How?"

"Because we are going to help you!"

"Why would you do that? You don't even know me!" Her voice caught at the end.

"Do you remember when you were a little girl before your mother died, you had a brother?"

"I didn't think I'd ever see him again. I was so young. I can barely remember him."

"Well, he remembers you," I told her. "He's here, in another tent, changing into one of those dumb white robes. We won't leave this place without you."

"Thank you," she whispered.

"What's all the noise in there?" A stern old woman's voice

interrupted us from outside the tent. "Don't speak to that girl. She is being punished!"

Yeah, really. She was beaten within an inch of her life, I thought grimly. "I'll be right out," I answered in my best cheerful tone. Then I whispered to Lydia, "Stay here. We'll be back later. I promise."

I had on my new "stylish" white robe now and prepared to join the stoned wackos out there. The games were about to begin.

Chapter 27

When I left the tent, I saw Charles across the flames of the bonfire and nearly burst out laughing. He was standing there, looking miserable in his long robe with the twine rope. He had his clothes and his favorite designer tie in his hands. I held my torn-up pink A-line dress.

"You may now throw your old clothes in the fire." I recognized the voice of the grouchy old woman who had admonished me not to speak to Lydia. Now, I got to see her in person. Her skin was brown and leathery, and her hair was in loose gray strands about her shoulders. Her faded blue eyes were tired but alert. She definitely wasn't on all the drugs the rest of the followers were.

"Remember—" she continued. "The discarding of your clothing symbolizes throwing away the things from your previous life. You are starting a new life now."

Yeah, as a drugged-up zombie, apparently, I thought, glimpsing the mere shadows of humans around me, dazed and incoherent. I casually tossed my clothes into the fire. Then I had to keep myself from smiling as Charles grimaced when he threw his beloved tie, along with the rest of his clothes, into the inferno.

"When you commit to us, remember it is forever. You are not bound to us by force but by choice. When you decide to become a part of us, you cannot break that vow. It is like a marriage binding your soul to ours."

What happens if I want a divorce, or even better, an annulment? Out loud, I said lightly, "What if, sometime in the future, we decide we want to leave?"

The old lady glared at me.

"No one ever wants to leave," she practically hissed between her teeth.

"How nice!" I politely responded. They probably shot deserters.

"I will now take you to meet your new master," the old woman said.

"And what is your name?" I asked.

"I am Juanita. The master is actually my son." I detected a strange sense of pride in her voice.

"What do you do here, Juanita?"

"I help initiate new members. I forage for food for our colony when needed. I take care of our master."

"Shouldn't he be taking care of you? Looks to me like he's a grown man."

"How dare you come here and criticize the way we live! Are you sure you really want to be here?"

"Of course, we want to be here. But don't you ever wonder about the things your son chooses to do, such as beating that poor girl in the tent for the 'sins' of the people here?"

"I do not question the actions of my son," Juanita said in a stony voice. "And neither should you. You need to put all of your energy into your initiation with us. Now that your clothes and your past have been destroyed, you may sit around the campfire and cohabit with your new family."

I sat down. Beside me was a girl with greasy dishwater blonde hair staring blindly into the fire. Charles sat on my other side, cross-legged and looking awkward in his new costume.

"Stay close to me," he said under his breath.

The sweet, heavy smell of marijuana filled the air.

I tried not to inhale it and held my breath for as long as I could until I couldn't stand it anymore. I was gasping for air. I gave up and sucked in all the oxygen I could.

The fire started getting hazy. The flames turned into different shapes and colors. They were suddenly fuchsia and aqua blue and light green. I reached out my hand, and my hand appeared as if there were a thousand of them. It was as if I was looking through a kaleidoscope. Then I tried to touch the pretty colors of the flames.

"Stop! You're going to hurt yourself!" Charles' faint voice called out.

I looked around. Where was he? I couldn't even see him. Then I turned around, and he was right there.

"Would you like to dance?" He was so tall, so devilishly handsome with that dark wavy hair and the silvery-blue eyes that haunted me ever since I had first seen him.

"How could I say no?" I stood up and put my hand in his.

"Katie, get back here!" I could hear Charles' voice in the background. I ignored it. This was the weirdest dream.

Charles put his hand around my waist and pulled me to him. We swayed in the smoke of the fire. Then he let me twirl around and come back to him.

"I never dreamed you were such a good dancer." I flirted with him.

"My new queen," he murmured.

What? I wondered hazily. That wasn't like something Charles would say. I looked at him closely. Suddenly, his beautiful dark locks of hair began to grow into long, filthy gray strands. His silvery-blue eyes faded into a murky gray. I shook my head in disbelief at the transformation. If I was dreaming, this was the worst dream ever.

Suddenly, I saw Damion's face fully before me. I had been dancing in his arms all along. I grimaced and shook his arms off me.

"Not so fast, my pretty. You are a natural in my arms." His rancid breath nearly knocked me over.

"I thought I was dancing with someone else!" I said between clenched teeth.

"Now, you will dance with no one else but me. I will make sure of that! My beauty! My queen!"

I rolled my eyes. What had I gotten myself into? This guy was a total freak.

"Let go of her!" Charles was struggling to free himself from the vise-like grip of several of the cult members who surrounded him now.

"Or you'll do what?" Damion laughed derisively. "You're in no position to make demands."

Unfortunately, he was right. We were in big trouble.

Chapter 28

I tried to use whatever was left of my superhuman strength to push Damion away from me. I shoved him hard enough (I thought) to knock him over. He didn't move.

I remembered Gabriel's words, "...the longer you stay, the more human you'll become." And I had been back on earth for quite a while now. My superhuman strength was all gone, just when I needed it most!

"I don't care what you do to me, but let her go, and I will stay with you forever!" Charles pleaded.

"I don't care whether you stay or go. It's her I want to marry, not you!"

"You just met her, you old pervert!"

I shook my head and tried to motion for Charles to shut up. There was nothing to be gained from incurring the wrath of Damion. Charles, however, wasn't paying any attention to me. I might have been a fly on the wall.

"This is my kingdom, and you are a mere peasant here."

"Some kingdom! A bunch of filthy tents set up here in the middle of nowhere with some drugged-up zombies for subjects!" Charles would not stop taunting him.

"I will not tolerate your disrespect!" Damion shouted. Then he turned back to me. "We will be married tonight, my love."

"No! Never!" Charles struggled to break free of Damion's minions, but to no avail.

"Take him out and kill him," Damion ordered. "He's ruining my festive mood." They started to drag Charles away into the darkness of the forest.

"Wait!" My voice cut through the air. "I will marry you of my own free will tonight if you let Charles go."

"You were going to marry me anyway tonight. That's not a good deal," Damion complained.

"What if I added to my vows tonight that I would love, obey, and serve you for the rest of my life?"

"Hmm...That does sound enticing!" His thin lips curved upward.

"Don't do it, Katie!" Charles called out.

"You could still kill Charles later if you'd like," I offered.

"Huh?" Charles was shocked. "Some guardian angel," he muttered.

"Let's leave him tied up during the ceremony. Then, in a few days, you could still kill him," I suggested. "It's in bad taste to murder on one's wedding day."

"I see your point! And I do want us to have a lovely ceremony tonight." He turned to the grisly druggies holding Charles. "Tie him up in one of the tents. Put a gag in his mouth, so I don't have to listen to him talk."

Poor Charles was struggling and turning his head from side to side, so they were having trouble getting that gag in his mouth. After gagging him, they finally managed to get him tied up and dragged him away into one of the tents.

I hated to leave him that way, but there was no alternative. I looked up at my new "fiancé," taking in his filthy stringy gray hair, his evil faded gray eyes, and leathery old skin. I just wanted to die. Except I was already practically dead.

Chapter 29

That evening, several women from the cult brushed my long hair, braided it, and twisted it up in a bun at the back of my neck. At least, I was getting a great hairdo out of all of this. I was quiet and said very little other than yes or no. I was playing the submissive, shy little bride-to-be part to the hilt.

An hour later, we started the ceremony. The cult members did this weird chanting as I walked slowly down the aisle. Damion's creepy mother was officiating.

They tied our hands together with a rope as part of the ceremony. They might as well have used poison ivy. I recited the vows I had made up about loving, serving, and obeying him for the rest of my life. As the words flowed through my lips, I felt a little sick to my stomach.

His mother, Juanita, pronounced us man and wife. He leaned in for a kiss. I leaned backward, away from him.

"Later—" I mouthed shyly. "When no one is watching." Later, as in maybe a million years.

The crowd let out a hoot and holler when they heard we were married. Damion tried to swoop me up in his arms and carry me down the aisle.

"Whoa, buddy...I can walk," I attempted what I hoped was an amiable grin.

"You are so pretty when you smile."

"Thank you," I answered.

He led me proudly inside his tent, which was bigger and better than the other ones.

"Why don't we have a toast to our marriage?" I suggested.

"Of course! I'll be right back." He disappeared for a few minutes. He brought back two plastic tumblers filled to the brim with some alcoholic beverage. "Sorry, I don't exactly have champagne glasses."

"That's all right."

We toasted our cups together. I pretended to take a sip but didn't. I loathed alcohol because I hated what it did to people. It made them lose control of their senses and usually made them do really stupid things they wouldn't otherwise do.

Damion downed the whole cup in two seconds, guzzling it like the pig he was. Then he poured himself some more. He offered some to me, but I shook my head, showing him that I still had plenty in my cup. I pretended to take another sip. He poured another cup down his throat. He drank like a fish. Within a few minutes, he was slurring his words and getting groggy. He finally collapsed in a corner and started snoring loudly.

I sat there watching him. When I was sure he was sleeping soundly, I crept to the opening of the tent and peeked out. No one was nearby. I saw some of the members lying down by the fire, but they were in drug-induced comas.

I crawled outside and went down to the tent where I had seen them drag Charles. I opened the flap and breathed a sigh of relief as I saw his eyes light up when he saw me. He was tied up in a corner with a gag still in his mouth.

I put my finger against my mouth, motioning for him not to make a sound. With one quick motion, I removed the gag.

"I knew you would come," he whispered.

I automatically threw my arms around him. I couldn't help myself. "The way you were acting, I was afraid you thought I really betrayed you," I said.

"I think I know you better than that by now," he grinned. "I knew you had a plan. I just didn't know what it was. By the way, you're not really married to that nut, are you?"

"Of course not! I never signed a marriage license, and his mother is not ordained as a minister. There is no way that ceremony was legal."

"Oh, good." Charles breathed a sigh of relief.

"Anyway, he's not my type. He's a little on the old side and definitely creepy." We laughed. "We've got to get out of here! Your sister is just two tents away." I worked on the knots tying his hands and feet together. The ropes around his feet were a tangled-up mess. I tried to unknot them with little success, so I switched back to the ropes around his hands. Finally, I was able to loosen them where his hands were free. Then he was quickly able to untie his feet. He jumped up.

"Now, time to get my sister away from this freak show!"

We opened the tent flap to sneak outside.

There, wouldn't you know it, was Juanita—my almost mother-in-law, standing there with a malevolent glint in her eyes and a sadistic smile.

"Where are you going so fast? Shouldn't you be with your new husband?"

"Get out of our way, or you'll be sorry," I said.

"We don't tolerate deserters." Her right hand had been behind her back. As she stepped closer, I could now see the gleaming of a dagger in her hand as she raised it to stab us to death.

Charles rushed forward and grabbed her right wrist and then wrestled her to the ground. They rolled in the grass, fighting for control of the knife. Juanita tried to claw Charles' face with her left hand, but he caught her wrist. After struggling for several minutes, he held her down. He managed to yank the knife out of her hand and throw it into the bushes. She was still kicking and screaming like a wild banshee—so much energy for a woman old enough to be a granny.

When she saw that she had lost, she said, "Go on and kill me then. I've lived long enough. Just make sure you do it quick."

Charles still held her down but said, "I'm not here to kill you, Juanita. I'm only here to get what's mine."

Her eyes narrowed, "What do you mean?"

"Never mind that. Katie—get the rope." I quickly picked it up and brought it to him. He tied up her feet and hands, even as she kept kicking and squirming. Then he carried her into the tent where he had been.

"You're a feisty old dame," he muttered. "And now, you can see how you like this gag." With one swift movement, he stuffed the gag in her mouth and tied a rag around her head. All the while, she was trying to bite him like a rabid animal. We left her there, squirming like a caterpillar trying to get out of a cocoon. At the tent entrance, I looked from one side to another and didn't see anyone awake. We quietly stepped outside.

"Hurry! She's waiting for us!" I whispered. We dashed toward Lydia's tent. Nervously, I opened the tent flap. Lydia was lying there asleep. Her back was to us.

"What are those bloody streaks on her back?" Charles asked.

"Damion beat her because she wouldn't marry him."

"That animal! I'll kill him!" he raged.

"Not a good idea. You'll end up in prison for the rest of your life. Trust God to repay him for what he's done. What we need to do is get Lydia out of here safely."

Lydia suddenly stirred. She turned over and looked up at us, specifically Charles.

"Who are you?" she asked as she gazed at him.

"I'm your brother, Charles. We've come to get you out of this place!" He knelt down and gently hugged her so as not to cause her any more pain. She threw her arms around him.

"I prayed to God that He would send someone to rescue me." Tears streamed down her face.

"I'm here now, Lydia. I won't leave you again," Charles promised her.

"Ah! What a sweet reunion!" Damion's voice snarled from behind. "Long-lost loves?"

"I'm her brother, you sicko, and she's leaving with me tonight!"

"Not if I have anything to say about it!" Damion lashed out at Charles with his whip but was startled when Charles caught it in his hand. Then Charles twisted it around his arm and yanked it away from him. In a quick move, he threw Damion to the ground and wrapped the whip around his neck.

I only hoped I could convince Charles not to kill Damion right then and there.

Chapter 30

"I could kill you this very minute if I wanted to. How does that make you feel, Damion?" Charles said.

"I'm not afraid to die. I will live eternally in heaven," Damion replied smugly.

"You are more than a little delusional, Damion. If I kill you now, you can find out right away if you made it to heaven!" Charles tightened the whip around Damion's neck.

"Remember who you are and Whose you are," I said softly to Charles. "You are not a killer."

"My fingers are just itching to tighten this whip around his neck."

I covered his hand with mine. "Let God take revenge."

Charles kept the whip around Damion's neck, and he leaned over until his mouth was next to Damion's ear.

"Do you hear that, Damion? God will take revenge on you for all of your evil deeds. Just remember every night when you go to sleep that God has seen every evil thing you've done. That includes you torturing my sister. You will be repaid!" Then he pulled the whip away quickly from Damion's neck and hit him once. Damion's head fell back to the ground as he lost consciousness.

"Did you have to hit him? Has everything I've taught you fallen by the wayside?" I rolled my eyes.

"I only hit him once to knock him out. We can't have that sicko following us."

"Violence is never the answer," I said.

Charles rolled his eyes, but I could see the glint of amusement in them. "Come on, Miss Perfect. Let's just get out of here while we still can. Hopefully, he'll be out for a few minutes."

"Yeah, if he's not dead already," I scoffed.

"That'll be the day!" Charles replied.

He put one arm around me and the other around his sister. We crept out of the tent, only to find Damion's wacko mother staring down at us with a smug look on her face. Beside her stood three beefy-looking male followers.

What a time for my superhuman strength to be missing in action.

"As I recall, I left you very tied up," Charles said with a puzzled expression on his face.

"As luck would have it, my son's loyal followers found me and untied me. Good for me, but not for you. We've been looking for you in every tent. Did you plan on leaving us so soon?" Juanita turned to her goons. "Tie them up. When Damion wakes up, he can decide how they will be executed."

The creepy cult guys started to drag us away.

"By the way, what is our precious little Lydia to you that you should go to so much trouble to get her away from us?" Juanita called out to Charles. "An old girlfriend, perhaps?"

"She's my sister, you witch, and I believe God sent me here to rescue her from you!" Charles told her.

"Soon, you will be dead. Where is your God now?" Her tone was mocking.

"I believe in Him, no matter what, even if we die!" Charles said.

"Drag them away," Juanita commanded. "I'm tired of looking at them!"

As we were being taken away, I whispered to Charles, "You really believe in God now?"

He smiled. "With every beat of my heart. He sent you to stop me from jumping off the roof, and now, he's reunited me with the sister I never thought I'd see again. Life is good."

"Even if you end up dying in a few hours?" I couldn't help asking.

"I don't believe life ends when I die anymore. It's only the beginning."

"Well, let's get you baptized first before you die," I suggested.

They tied us all up together and then left us.

"Charles?" Lydia said quietly.

"Yes?" he answered.

"There is a knife hidden in my pocket. Can you wiggle your hand around and get it out? Then, if you can cut me loose, I'll do the same for you, and then Katie."

"How did you get a knife?" I asked.

"When you two weren't looking, I went back to Damion's tent after he fell asleep drunk and found it. I thought we might need it later as a plan B."

"I have a brilliant sister," Charles grinned.

"I know," Lydia replied.

Charles squeezed his hands around and got the knife out of Lydia's robe pocket. Then he started cutting her ropes. Within a few minutes, she was free. Then, she, in turn, cut Charles' ropes. He jumped up and helped Lydia up as well.

"Maybe, we should leave her here," Charles said, looking down at me.

"I'm not staying with these nuts," I said.

Charles bent down, working on cutting the knots of my ropes.

"As if I'd leave the other half of me here," he said in a low voice that I almost couldn't hear.

Soon, we were all free and more than ready to leave. We dashed out. Charles carried Lydia in his arms because she could barely walk. Surprisingly, no one was watching. Maybe this time, our escape would actually happen.

The night was still bright because of the full moon, but we had to go slowly, so we wouldn't trip over bushes, sticks, or branches. It seemed like it took us forever to get back to our car, and all the while, we were straining our ears, listening for our captors.

After what seemed like hours, we made it back to the clearing. The moon shone down on Charles' car since there were no trees directly over it to block the light. We were about fifty feet away from the safety that our car could provide us.

And that is when we heard them. A sound like the cries of wild animals swept through the forest. We had been discovered, and they were coming after us for one reason: to kill us all.

Chapter 31

"Hurry!" I whispered to Charles.

We walked as fast as we could, halfway running to the car. We could only go so fast since Charles was still carrying Lydia.

I ran ahead, tripping ungracefully over a stick hidden in the tall grass. I used Charles' key that he had kept hidden in his robe pocket to open the front and back car doors. Charles was just a few steps behind me. He carefully laid Lydia in the backseat. Then he and I quickly jumped into the front seat.

We hadn't even closed the car doors when the entire cult started running into the clearing after us. Several had torches on long brown branches. In their flowing white robes, they resembled a bunch of ghoulish ghosts. We slammed the doors shut as they started running toward us. Then, we banged on the car door locks to make sure they couldn't get in.

With the slip of his hand, Charles jammed the key into the

ignition and turned it. The car sputtered but didn't start.

The crazed cult members were all around our car screaming unintelligible gibberish like a bunch of rabid dogs. They were beating on the car and attempting to unlock the doors.

I knew of only one thing to do. I started praying.

I called out to the only One who could help us. "God, I know You're watching over us. Please deliver us from these evil people. Please let the car start. In Jesus' name, Amen."

The ignition clicked. The Mustang roared to life, and Charles floored the gas pedal. The car jerked forward. Two burly cult members jumped on the front hood of the car. Charles sped ahead, not able to see too well because they were up against the windshield, screaming and beating against the glass.

Charles started to zigzag the car to the right and left, all the while going really fast. One man fell off and crashed into a tree. The other held on for dear life.

"Can you drive for a few minutes?" Charles asked me.

"Why? Are you going somewhere?" I asked. The last thing I wanted was to drive with this crazy nut job attached to the front of Charles' car.

"Just do what I say. Take over now!" Charles commanded.

I scooted over in the blink of an eye.

Charles climbed over me to my seat and rolled the window down. He stood up in the seat with the rest of his body sticking out the window. He grabbed the man by his robe. When the cult member tried to put his hands around Charles' neck, Charles punched him with his other hand. The man's head bobbed back. In a split second, while the guy was caught off guard, Charles shoved him off the car into some bushes.

The human part of me hoped that bush had a lot of thorns.

Charles got back into the car.

"Good work! I couldn't have done better myself!" I bragged on him.

"I never want to be anywhere near another cult for the rest of my life!" Charles said.

"You and me both!" I agreed. "By the way, is there anywhere in particular you want me to drive us?"

"No. Just keep driving, though!" Charles said. "I want as much space between us and that cult as possible!"

"I second that," I replied.

We drove about three more hours and decided to stop in Springfield, Missouri.

First, we went to a medical clinic where they cleaned and bandaged Lydia's wounds on her back from the beating. Then, we drove around looking for a hotel where we could rest for a few days and Lydia could recuperate. We chose a colorful retro 1950s place called Route 66 Motel. It had neon pink and green letters that blinked every few seconds on a sign that said there were still rooms available. There was a brick one-level long stretch of motel rooms with plenty of cars parked in front of them. It was clearly safe and very welcoming.

After checking in, we situated Lydia in one of the double beds in our room, and then we went to JCPenney and Sears for some normal-looking clothes. I was sick of looking like a cult member, and my old clothes were still at Paula's house.

Luckily, Lydia and I were about the same size, so I found us a couple of pairs of bell-bottom jeans, some peasant blouses, and several dresses. I also had to buy us other necessary things like makeup and shoes. I guess the makeup wasn't necessary, but Lydia deserved a pick-me-up, and I really wanted a new tube of pink lipstick.

Charles was forced to shop for himself unless he wanted to walk around in a white robe. I helped him pick out some dress pants, a couple of suits, some jeans, a few T-shirts, some dress shirts, and two designer ties to replace the one he was forced to throw in the fire. We changed into some of our new normal clothes in the changing rooms while we were still at one of the stores. He was in black dress pants and a white long-sleeved dress shirt. I was in a turquoise dress with an empire waist and white sandals. It was great to look human again.

Next, we drove around looking for somewhere to eat. Charles finally settled on Denny's, a restaurant which mainly sold American fare such as—you guessed it—juicy cheeseburgers. That was my only requirement—that wherever we ate, they had to have cheeseburgers.

Charles opened the car door for me and the doors to the restaurant. There was always an air of gentlemanly chivalry about him that I loved. None of the men I had known in the twenty-first century had been like that.

Charles pulled out the chair at our table for me to sit in. Then he sat down across from me. We ordered iced tea.

"What do you want? A cheeseburger?" Charles asked.

"Yes!" I nodded eagerly. "With onions, tomatoes, lettuce, pickles, and mayonnaise. The works!" Time for a little reward for escaping from that crazy cult and saving Lydia in the process.

As I sat there, resting my eyes on Charles' gorgeous face, it seemed hard to believe that just a short time ago, we had been tied up together in a tent, waiting to be massacred.

Charles ordered a cheeseburger for me and then a steak for himself. After the waitress was gone, his face turned serious.

"I've never been so happy." His eyes were warm as he gazed at me.

"You are homeless, barely have a few clothes and your car, are still on the lam from the mobsters, and you nearly just got whacked by some drugged-up cult members...and you're happy?"

"None of that matters because I have you."

"But only for a short time. I can't stay forever."

"If you could, would you?"

"Maybe...Probably...Oh, good grief...What's the point of lying? You know I would," I admitted.

"Couldn't you ask them to change the rules up there?"

"What if I want to see my family again? I've known you for only a few weeks, but I knew them for twenty-one years."

"I feel like I've known you all my life," he replied softly. His eyes were piercing, and I could feel myself drowning in them.

"I wish I could stay, but I've got a place I've got to go, and you've got the rest of your life ahead of you. Someday, you'll marry and have children. You'll forget all about me." I laughed a little nervously. Did I really *want* him to forget about me?

"I could never forget you. Even if I marry, as you say I will someday, yours is the face I will dream about every night."

"Then I feel sorry for your wife," I grinned sarcastically. Maybe I was trying to hurt him for making me feel something.

The waitress brought a huge, juicy cheeseburger with french fries and set it all in front of me. My mouth was watering at the sight of it. She also brought Charles his steak.

I held my cheeseburger for a few seconds, staring at it like it was a sacred treasure. Then I ate a huge bite of it, closed my eyes in reverie, and enjoyed the taste of it—the melted cheddar cheese melded with the charred meat mixed with the other ingredients—all of it was sheer perfection.

I opened my eyes, only to find Charles watching me intently.

"I love watching you eat. You savor each bite as if it was your very first or as if you'll never get to eat it again."

"They might not have cheeseburgers in heaven."

"I'd make sure you got them all the time if you stayed with me."

"That's bribery! Totally unfair!" I protested.

"Haven't you heard 'all's fair in love and war'?"

"That's just an old saying used to excuse all kinds of atrocities."

"Like my using cheeseburgers to bribe you to stay here?"

"Exactly." I could feel my face turning red—time to change the subject. "By the way, when are you going to get baptized? Surely, you must realize from all the danger we've been in recently how fragile life is. I want to make sure you're saved, just in case those awful gangsters do succeed in killing you."

"I love how positive you are."

"Not positive. Just realistic."

"Do you think I'm ready to be baptized?"

"You said you believe in God, right?"

"Yes, I do now."

"Do you believe Jesus Christ is the Son of God?"

"Absolutely."

"Then you are ready. But just to make sure, why don't we spend the next three days studying the Bible? Let's also pray about it and ask God to give you clarity in your decision."

"That sounds like a plan."

We ate the rest of our food and enjoyed each other's company. It was like we were celebrating after escaping from the cult and rescuing Lydia from Damion's clutches. I felt so relaxed with him and completely free to be myself. It was easy to pretend that I would be with him always.

Chapter 32

When we got back to the hotel, I intended to talk with Lydia about our plans for the next few days. I wanted to see where she was spiritually and hopefully get her on board for studying the Bible with Charles and me. Charles had gone out again to run some errands, and we were alone in the hotel room.

I don't know why, but I felt nervous talking to her about Jesus, God, and her spirituality. I guess one reason was that I didn't know her that well. However, the biggest reason was that I wasn't used to talking to people about God. I felt ashamed of myself. When I was alive, I had talked a lot, but not about what mattered most.

Lydia was lying in bed, reading.

"Uh, Lydia?" I started. Could I make this any more awkward?

She looked up from her book.

"Yes, Katie?"

"Just wanted to ask, are you a Christian?" The room was quiet, and I wondered if she had heard me or was furious and thought I was being nosy.

"I am. I was baptized nine years ago. My relationship with God is what got me through being a captive in the cult. I even tried to share my faith with Damion and his mother."

"You did?" Her bravery amazed me. "What was their reaction?"

"That was the first time they got really angry at me and beat me. They already had their own version of religion—if that's what you'd call it—inside their own heads. They didn't want to hear the truth."

"I've never met anyone who was actually beaten for sharing his or her faith."

"It was a small price to pay to try and reach them and share God's love with them. When I saw they weren't receptive, I prayed to God to send someone to rescue me from them, and He did."

"I couldn't be happier that we were the ones God chose to help you escape. Now, I was wondering if you could help me with something..."

"Anything. All you have to do is ask."

I told her that Charles was close to being baptized. I asked her if she could study the Bible with us over the next few days and pray with us.

"How exciting! There's nothing that makes me happier than leading someone to Christ! And my own brother! When can we start?"

"Oh, I'm so glad! I was hoping you'd feel that way!" I said.

When Charles came back, Lydia and I met him at the door with jubilant faces.

"Okay. What's going on? You two look like you've just shared the best secret in the world."

"Actually, it is. And soon, you'll know it too," Lydia said cheerfully.

"You can enlighten me any time. What have you been talking about?"

"The love of God," Lydia answered. "And how you need to learn more about Him."

Lydia led Charles to the small night table. Then she got out the Bible that was in the drawer and laid it in front of him.

"In this Book, you'll find all the answers you'll ever need in this life and the life to come," she told him.

That was when I realized I had found in her the perfect co-conspirator in helping me to guide Charles on his spiritual journey.

The next few days were some of the best in my existence. Charles, Lydia, and I poured over the four Gospels and also studied other parts of the Bible together, discussing the stories and lessons. Then, we would pray for more understanding. Charles was astounded by the wisdom of the Proverbs. He also loved the Sermon on the Mount in Matthew 5-7. His heart and mind were open. He had fascinating insights and interesting questions. Lydia and I prayed for God to guide us as we did our best to answer his questions. It was times like this that made me wish I had been more of a Bible scholar when I was alive and had the chance. Hopefully, now I was starting to make up for it.

After several days of intense study, Charles, Lydia, and I felt he was ready to be baptized. I looked through the phone book and found a Bible-based church several streets away from our hotel. I called the office there and spoke to a church secretary and told her we needed their preacher to baptize Charles. She told us to come directly to their building. Then we could speak to their preacher, Ray Holloway, who happened to be there that day, studying his notes for the sermon on Sunday.

"What should I wear?" Charles wondered. I could tell he was nervous.

"Whatever you want. God doesn't have a dress code." I couldn't help but smile. Charles hardly ever got nervous about anything.

When I saw him a few minutes later, he was in his new beautiful black suit we picked out from Sears.

"I wanted to put on the best thing I had for the Lord," he declared.

"You look...great." I fumbled over the words as I gazed at him admiringly. His dark, thick hair was brushed back from his face, and his silvery-blue eyes were sparkling. He looked like a movie star.

Lydia came up behind us. "Time to go, everyone!" she announced and opened the door.

The church secretary had given us extensive directions, even though it was only about five minutes away. We turned into the parking lot.

It was a medium-sized brick building with steps leading to glass doors. It had a white steeple above it. The windows were stained glass with all the colors of the rainbow.

We rang a doorbell, and a gray-haired black woman with a kind face opened the door for us.

"Hi! I'm Ruby. I'm so happy you came to us today!" She warmly welcomed us and invited us to come inside.

We introduced ourselves, and Charles indicated that he was the one who wanted to be baptized.

"What a fine young man you are! And you have made the very best decision of your life!" She patted his shoulder. She reminded me of my grandmother, who had showered me with love all throughout my childhood.

"Thank you, ma'am. I appreciate that more than you know," Charles answered.

Ruby had us sit down on a wooden bench in the hallway while she ran to get the preacher.

Ray Holloway, the preacher, was about six feet tall with thick brown hair, gray eyes, and a commanding presence. He gave us each a firm handshake. He paused when he saw Charles.

"So, you are the one who wants to be baptized and become a Christian?" Ray asked.

"Yes, sir. My sister and my friend here, who are already baptized, have been studying the Bible with me for several days. I want more than anything in the world to become a Christian."

"Do you believe that Jesus Christ is the Son of God and repent of your sins?"

"Yes, I do," Charles answered.

"With that confession, I believe you are ready for baptism. Do you want to be baptized now or next Sunday in front of the congregation?"

"Right now, sir. I don't want to waste another minute."

The preacher chuckled. "If only the rest of the world could be like you, my job would be finished. Come with me, young man, and I'll help you get ready."

They headed down the hall. Ruby came back to us and led Lydia and me to the auditorium. When we got there, I looked around. The rays of the sun reached through the stained-glass windows and made the colors glow all over the light blue carpet. The effect was mesmerizing.

"Would you mind if I watch Charles' baptism with you?" Ruby asked us. "I always enjoy watching one of God's children being saved."

"Of course," Lydia told her. "It would be an honor."

So, we sat together on one of the long wooden pews at the front of the auditorium and waited in excited anticipation.

After a few minutes, I could hear the swishing of the water in the baptistery. I then heard the squeaking of the dark blue curtains as the preacher pulled on the cord and opened them, so we could view the baptism. Then I saw the preacher and Charles in the water. Charles was in a white robe, and Ray was in a white dress shirt with black suspenders, probably wearing his signature outfit that he reserved especially for these occasions.

After a moment of silence, the preacher spoke. "Do you believe Jesus is the Son of God, and do you repent of your sins?"

"Yes, I do," Charles responded.

"Since you have confessed that Jesus Christ is the Son of God, I now baptize you in the name of Jesus Christ, God, and the Holy Ghost for the remission of your sins." Then the preacher dipped Charles into the water.

I heard the water splash as Charles went under and then it splashed even bigger an instant later when he came back up.

The preacher put his arm around him warmly and patted him on the back.

"Congratulations, you are now a Christian!" Ray's booming voice filled the church.

Charles looked down at us, and a beaming smile stretched across his face from ear to ear. He looked different to me somehow. There was a special glow about him. I could only describe his face as radiant.

Lydia squeezed my hand, and our eyes met. Her eyes were full of happy tears, but at the same time, I could tell she was bubbling over with excitement. Even Ruby had tears in her eyes, and she didn't even know Charles.

I had to ask myself, why hadn't I cared like this when I was alive every time a Christian was baptized? I had no answer and no excuse.

A few minutes later, Charles came out, still glowing. All three of us ran to him and hugged him.

"I am so happy for you!" I told him.

"Thank you! And I appreciate you and Lydia taking the time to study the Bible with me the past few days!" Charles said. "If it weren't for you two, I would still be the person I was before."

"We didn't do it. God did," Lydia said. "He must have a bright future planned for you!"

"Whatever He has planned for me in the future, I accept all of it with an open and willing heart," he replied.

"I want you to know I'll be praying for you!" Ruby said, clasping his hand in hers. Then she smiled at us. "Would you all like to come to my house for dinner to celebrate?"

"You will have been at work all day. Won't you be too tired? We couldn't possibly impose on you like that," Charles protested.

"Impose? What an insult! Now that you are a Christian, you are part of my family. Family never imposes! I won't take no for an answer. And I'm a great cook!" She winked at us.

"If you insist," Charles said.

"I do!" Ruby answered. "It'll be like a party, and I'm a party girl at heart." She looked up at the preacher. "And you are invited too! Don't even think of saying no!"

"I know better than to say no to you, Ruby Wells!" The preacher let out a loud belly laugh. "Don't worry; I'll be there." Then he hugged Ruby.

That night at Ruby's, we feasted on roast beef, baked potatoes, macaroni and cheese, squash casserole, and green beans with chocolate cake and homemade ice cream for dessert. Ruby didn't lie about her cooking abilities. It was one of the best meals I ever had. Her husband and grandkids were there too and were just as warm as her.

Ray presented Charles with a black leather Bible after dinner. "Everything you need to keep Satan away is in this Book," the preacher told him.

"But you just met me, and now you're giving me this?" Charles was surprised.

"Among Christians, there are no strangers," Ray said. "Just friends we haven't met."

"Thank you so much, Ray. I assure you I'll be reading this Book a lot."

"I have no doubt," Ray patted him on the back. "We give all of our newborns in Christ a Bible to keep. Be sure and mark it up. Underline your favorite verses, the ones that inspire you the most. Make it yours. Use it as a tool to communicate with God. Don't let it gather dust. Wear it out."

"Don't worry, Ray. It won't get dusty," Charles grinned as he shook Ray's hand.

I was so happy as we headed back to our motel. Ruby, her family, and Ray had been so kind not only to Charles but to Lydia and me as well. The whole day had left a glow in my heart. I almost wished I could stay forever in this town with Charles and Lydia.

But surely, my job here was done. Charles wasn't suicidal anymore. There was no sign of the thugs from the mob following us. Charles was reunited with his sister. And he was no longer an atheist; he was a newborn Christian! I imagined those pearly gates would be opening up for me any moment now!

As much as I hated to leave Charles and Lydia, I was looking forward to seeing my family again. And I really felt I deserved a reward for all that I had gone through. I mean, I had gotten shot at! Definitely not at the top of my list of fun things to do.

I lay awake that night, waiting for something spectacular to happen, like maybe a lightning bolt zapping me into the sky.

But nothing happened.

And finally, I fell asleep.

Chapter 33

I was dreaming about eating another delicious meal at Ruby's. We were all eating cheeseburgers with fries this time. I was just about to take the first big juicy bite out of mine when I looked across the table and saw Gabriel sitting there with a hint of a smile on his face.

"Gabriel, this is *my* dream! Can't I just enjoy a bite of my favorite food on earth?" I asked.

"Sure. I'm not stopping you," he replied.

I put down my sandwich. It was as big as my hands.

"I can't eat this with you staring at me."

"Well, then, don't. It's not like you're eating a real cheeseburger anyway."

His suggestion settled into my subconscious mind. I looked down. The burger vanished.

"Hey, wait a minute—" I protested. What did I have to do to make it come back?

"We've got to talk," Gabriel announced.

"I'll say. Why am I not in paradise right now? Haven't I been through enough?" I tried to keep the irritated tone out of my voice but probably failed miserably.

"God's timetable is different from yours," he said simply.

"So, how long do I have to stay? Years, decades, forever?"

"That—" Gabriel suddenly glared at me ferociously, "is not for you to know!"

"I'm sorry." I was suddenly meek again. There was no way I was arguing with an angel.

His face softened immediately.

"Do you really hate it here so much?" he asked.

"No, it's not that. Maybe, I'm getting to like it here too much. And like Charles too much. I don't want to be completely happy here, only to have it all ripped away from me when I have to leave."

My answer caught me off guard. I didn't even know I felt that way until I said it.

"Your problem is that you are focusing too much on yourself. Focus on helping Charles and his sister instead, and you'll be just fine."

Before I could protest, he continued. "And now, I have another assignment for you..."

I swallowed hard and nodded. I had already made up my mind that whatever he asked, I would do it. I was a little worried though. What if I didn't succeed this time? I could lose everything, maybe even my very soul.

Chapter 34

I woke up still tired. Often these days, even when I was asleep, I wasn't really resting. Once again, Gabriel had invaded my dreams. And with all my superhuman power MIA, I was feeling like just another grouchy human who hadn't gotten enough sleep. Lydia came bouncing into my corner of our hotel room.

"Good morning!" she called out.

"Is it?" I pulled the covers back over my head and turned over. I didn't feel like being a guardian angel today. My eyes closed, and I went back to sleep.

A couple of hours later, I was feeling a bit perkier. The smell of bacon and eggs filled the room. I opened my eyes.

Lydia was heading toward me from the kitchenette with a tray piled high with breakfast food. Browned bacon, fluffy scrambled eggs, and sausage and biscuits met my eyes.

"Here! This'll make you human again!" she said.

"Yeah, that would be great—if I was human," I retorted.

She gave me a strange look.

"What do you mean?"

"Nothing. Don't worry about it," I said quickly. What was I doing, making stupid, cryptic remarks like that? Maybe, the strain of this whole situation was starting to get to me. I settled down and began to eat ravenously. The bacon was crisp and well done, just as I liked it. The eggs were moist. I could tell she put butter and cheese in them, and the biscuits with the spicy sausage melted in my mouth. It was easy to tell the biscuits were homemade. I was starting to feel better already. Charles happened to be out running errands again, so it was just Lydia and me.

"Where did you learn to cook like that?" I managed to say between bites of food. "You're incredible."

"My adoptive parents taught me," she said matter-of-factly.

"What was your life like growing up?" I asked.

"It wasn't always so great. After I was taken from Charles at the orphanage, I was switched from family to family for years. A few of them were physically abusive. Some of them only had me there because of the money they got from the government as foster parents. But this couple finally did adopt me when I was twelve. I lived with them until I was seventeen."

"What happened then?"

"They died in a plane crash. They had no relatives, so the government tried to put me back into an orphanage. I decided I wasn't going and ran away. Since then, I've been a bit of a vagrant. I had several waitressing jobs, some bad apartments, and even worse boyfriends.

"But throughout my life, ever since my adoptive parents taught me about God, I've had a close relationship with Him. I knew He'd take care of me. When I was a captive, living in the cult, I knew God would see me through. Even if I died there, it was a win-win situation because then I'd get to go to heaven. But then, He sent you and Charles to rescue me, so He must have a purpose for me to stay on this earth a while longer."

Her faith in God astounded me. I was shocked into silence, which was pretty unusual. No wonder I hadn't quite made it to heaven. This woman's faith was leaps and bounds ahead of mine when I had been alive.

"I wish I could be more like you," I finally said.

"What are you saying? You helped convert Charles! He was an atheist before he met you!"

"I don't take credit for that. That was all God's doing." I left out the part that I hadn't really had a choice about helping Charles and that I had been unexpectedly been thrown into his life.

"Whatever the circumstances were in your coming into Charles' life, you are just what he needed. God must have known that when He sent you to him. You know Charles is in love with you, don't you?"

"I know." Her words hit me like a ton of bricks or a knife right through my heart. Yes, I knew.

"And you love him too. I've seen the way you look at him."

I couldn't deny that, so instead, I turned away. I could feel the tears filling my eyes.

"You could marry him someday, Katie. You would both be so happy. I can see it all now!" She came up behind me, her voice full of joy. "You and I would be best friends, of course. I'd eventually get married and live close by. We could raise our kids together. Charles and I would have the family we never had. We could even live in a big house all together!"

It sounded like *The Waltons* or some crazy version of *The Brady Bunch*. I didn't say that out loud since those shows hadn't even come out yet. The picture she painted of our future was rosy though. I brushed away my tears. I wouldn't get to be a part of it.

"I can't stay with you and Charles," I said quietly. She might as well know that right now and not get her hopes up.

"Why?" Then her eyes got wide. "Are you already married?"

I almost laughed at her doe-eyed innocence. She was adorable.

"No. It's nothing like that. I don't think I'm allowed to tell you the reasons I can't stay. I was only meant to remain with you and Charles for a short time to help you, and then I'll be gone."

"God sent you to us, didn't He?"

There was an ethereal quality to her demeanor as if she had a sixth sense. It was no use lying to her.

"Yes, you could say that..."

"Are you an angel?"

"Well...not technically..."

"I knew there was something special about you!" She threw her arms around me.

"Please..." I rolled my eyes. "I'm not that special." I didn't even have any superhuman power anymore. I was just a regular, almost boring, girl next door now.

"Everyone is special in God's eyes! And He must have seen something in you to allow you to help us! Charles told me you stopped him from committing suicide."

"I don't take credit for that. God did that, not me..."

"But you were a part of that miracle!" she insisted.

"Only a very small part." What was wrong with me? When I was alive, I'd wanted to take one hundred percent credit for everything good imaginable. My ego had been through the roof. This whole experience of being a guardian angel had changed me without me even realizing it. Now, I was giving the credit to God, the One to whom I should have given it all along.

Chapter 35

When Charles got back to our hotel room, I realized I needed to start the next part of our journey. I was painfully aware that Gabriel and God were watching me every minute. I didn't have forever to complete each assigned task.

I pulled Charles and Lydia aside and told them we needed to have a meeting.

"Why? You're not leaving us, are you?" Lydia's eyes were wide and full of dismay. Charles shot me a tortured look.

"No!" I quickly reassured them. "It's nothing like that! But we do need to be moving on soon."

"Did you see the hitmen again?" Charles asked.

"No. As far as I know, they are not on our trail anymore."

"Wow. That's such a relief!" Lydia paused for a moment, thinking. "Why don't we just stay together in Springfield? I like it here. We could make a life for ourselves in a place like this."

She was right. Everything we could ever need was in this small beautiful town. We would have a wonderful church to be a part of with the kind preacher who baptized Charles. The people here were warm and down-to-earth. Also, the pace of life was slower here than in a big city like New York or Chicago. In the farmland that was just a few minutes outside of town, the sky seemed never-ending. In that open land, there were no electric wires or tall skyscrapers to mar the view when you looked up. It was definitely Big Sky Country.

"I'm not saying you can't ever come back to Springfield, but there is somewhere we need to go now."

"Where are you getting your orders?" Charles asked.

I looked up.

"Then we'll go wherever He wants us to go," Charles said.

"We're going to see your father," I announced.

165

"What? I thought he was dead! I haven't seen him for over twenty years. I wouldn't even know how to find him!" Charles said.

"I do," I replied.

"How?" he demanded.

"I have connections...Remember how we found your sister?" I reminded him. How quickly he forgot that this was not a normal situation. If it were, it might take weeks, months, or even years to find his father. But with God, anything was possible.

"Could you just ask Him if we can skip finding my father? I don't really care about seeing him again," Charles said. The pain clearly registered in his eyes.

"Speak for yourself! I'd like to track him down and ask why Mama had to take us and run away from him all those years ago. He must've been a monster!" Lydia grimaced. Then she thought a moment and added, "Maybe you are right, Charles, about not wanting to see him again."

"But we have to go see him," I told them. "We're not saying no to God."

"Oh, all right!" Charles glowered. "Just don't expect me to be happy about it! If I never saw that man till the day I died, it would be too soon!"

There was an awkward silence in the room.

"All right, then! Let's go pack!" I said cheerfully.

They both glared at me and said nothing.

Chapter 36

Gabriel told me that their father would be in Carthage, a town about an hour from Springfield. The best way to get there was to drive on Route 66.

I was so excited! We were taking a road trip on the famous Mother Road of the USA! We were able to pack our things pretty fast since we didn't have much. As we were walking to the car, Charles turned to me.

"Why don't you drive? I never wanted to see my father again, and I still don't. I'll just stay in the back seat and sleep."

"Are you kidding me?" I looked at him incredulously. "We are getting to take a road trip on Route 66! I don't want you to miss it! You're driving!"

"I've done everything you ever wanted me to do. Everything... but this." He turned away from me.

"Where's your trust in God? He'll work everything out," I assured him.

"Do you really believe that?"

"I wouldn't say it if I didn't. Besides, it's not like you're going alone to see your father. Lydia is with you, and I am too. We're a team! So, let's try to have some fun on our road trip!"

He finally turned back to me and grinned, and his smile was like a rainbow shining through the dark clouds.

"I have always wanted to drive on Route 66," he admitted.

"Well, there you go! Here's your chance!" I said. "And you've got to take advantage of each chance when it comes along because it might not happen again!"

"Well said!" Lydia piped up behind me. "Now, put on your sunglasses, and let 'er rip!"

We piled in the car. Lydia was in the backseat with Charles and me in the front. He put down the top on the convertible. We all were wearing our sunglasses. When he started the car, I flipped on the radio, and the Beach Boys were singing "Surfin' U.S.A." It was a perfect song for our carefree mood.

Charles drove about forty miles an hour, slow enough so that he could enjoy the scenery too. There was so much to see: quaint old wooden fences surrounding lush farms, dilapidated barns you can see the sky through, beautiful horses with their tails swaying gracefully in the wind, and cows grazing on the grass, soaking up the afternoon sun. Soon, we arrived at a ghost town named Spencer. It still had two abandoned gas pumps in front of a small set of run-down buildings and faded letters that said "Feed Store" on one of the windows. No one was there but us. Charles stopped the car, and we got out. I had never been to a ghost town before. The only sounds I could hear were birds chirping and the trickle of water rushing over rocks at a nearby creek. Charles happened to have a camera, and Lydia wanted to take a picture of us.

We posed beside the faded red gas pumps.

"Get closer and act like you like each other!" Lydia called out.

I scooted toward him awkwardly, keeping my eyes on the ground.

"It's okay. I won't hurt you," he whispered into my ear.

I slowly crept closer to him. I felt his arm slide around my waist so naturally as if he did this all the time. He pulled me gently toward him. Shivers ran up and down my back. I don't even know if I was smiling when Lydia snapped the picture. All I could think of was—him and how I wished this moment would never end.

"Great picture, Katie!" Lydia announced. "By the way, I've never seen you look so happy before! It's going to be a beautiful photograph!" She had a sly smile on her face.

I felt the redness creeping up my neck and into my face.

"There! That wasn't so hard, was it?" Charles gave me a quick squeeze and then let me go.

I rolled my eyes at him and then looked away. Actually, he had no idea how hard it was: to be so close to everything I wanted, to have his arm around me like that, and then to have it end in a split second. Yeah, I'll have to admit, it put me in a foul mood. And guardian angels weren't supposed to be moody. But this one sure was! I turned to Lydia.

"I'll take some shots of you with Charles now!" I volunteered. At least, then I wouldn't have to feel his arm around me and be tempted to think of him in ways I shouldn't.

Charles and Lydia stood beside an old café window that was partly shattered. I didn't have to tell them to stand close together, smile, or even pose. They looked so natural together and at ease. You'd never guess they had been separated for over two decades and had just recently been reunited.

Charles had his arm protectively around Lydia's shoulders. She leaned her head against him. You could tell they would do anything for each other. And they looked like they were related too: the thick, dark hair with the olive complexion. And then, there were those identical silvery-blue eyes that both of them had. The eyes almost made you do a double-take when you first saw them, as strikingly beautiful as they were.

I took several pictures of them posing in various places around the ghost town: beside the feed store, the general store, and around the old gas station. I couldn't help myself. They looked so good together, and I knew these pictures would be treasured by them years later as a reminder of the time when they found each other again. I took a picture of them by the Spencer town sign, on the steel-barred covered bridge over the creek, and beside some of the forest that surrounded the small abandoned town.

While Lydia was out picking some wildflowers, I decided to snap a picture of Charles. He had been sitting on a sagging porch, resting for a few minutes. When I moved the camera in his direction, I caught him in an unguarded moment. His eyes had been following me. There was a wistful sadness in them that clinched at my heart—a secret longing for something he could never have.

I drew in a sharp breath, and it caught in my throat. I wondered if every man was as much of an open book as Charles or if I was just that good at reading him. And I felt the very same way he did. Only, I had to try and hide it because there was absolutely nowhere it could go.

I went and sat beside him, trying to be cheerful and perky like Lydia. "You didn't smile for the picture!" I needled him.

"I don't always feel like smiling, Katie."

"Why?"

"You know why. Don't pretend that you don't know. I can't ever get you out of my mind. It would be easier if I didn't see you every waking hour, but I do! You're everywhere! Now, you torment me in my sleep as well. Even in my dreams, you won't leave me alone!"

"Well, I hope they aren't nightmares!" I said flippantly, trying in vain to lighten his mood.

"They're far from nightmares, Katie!" He gripped my arm with his hand earnestly. "They're more like visions of the kind of life we could have together. Do you know we could be happy anywhere if we were together? We were happy in Nashville, the Kentucky countryside near Wickliffe, Springfield, and now on Route 66. I was even happy looking for the cult in the middle of the Mark Twain Forest because you were with me, and I think you feel the same way about me. I know you do because I can feel it." He placed my hand over his heart. "Here."

My hand started sliding from his chest to around his neck; my lips were just mere inches from his.

"I'm so tired of trying to resist you," I said to him softly.

"Then stop trying," he said under his breath. His own arm had crept around my neck too. So easily.

Our lips touched, and it was like fireworks again. My eyes closed, and it was as if I were in a dream, a perfect one. He held me there so tenderly as if I was a piece of porcelain china. If I ever had any doubts about how he might have felt about me, they were all gone.

"Help!" Lydia shrieked. She was running up the street as a swarm of yellow jackets chased her. "I'm allergic to bees!"

"Oh, no!" Charles said as he started racing toward her. The car was several yards away. For the first time, I wished it wasn't a convertible.

Charles practically leaped toward Lydia and, in an instant, swept her up in his arms and carried her as if she was as light as a baby, running like crazy to the car.

"Get in!" He managed to tell me in a raspy voice as he dumped Lydia into the back seat. Then he jumped over the side door and into his seat. I was in the car in a matter of seconds.

The yellow jackets were starting to swirl angrily around us. I was swatting at them with my hands. Charles was having trouble starting the engine.

"Please, God, let the engine start...Please get us out of here!" I prayed in the name of Jesus.

Two seconds later, we heard the engine rumble to life. Charles jerked the shift into drive, and we roared off.

"Thank you, God!" I whispered.

Miles down the road, after we were safe again, Lydia commented, "No wonder that place is a ghost town. The yellow jackets probably killed everyone!"

We laughed. But then we solemnly agreed that it would be a long time before we visited Spencer again.

Chapter 37

Before we knew it, we were in Carthage. We passed one Victorian mansion after another. The streets were tree-lined and shady. I'll have to say it was the most breathtaking place I'd ever seen.

"So, do we know where my father's house is?" Charles was looking around intently as he drove. I could tell he was nervous.

"Let me get back to you on that. For now, just keep on driving." I closed my eyes and hoped Gabriel was listening. *Gabriel, are you there?*

"You don't have to close your eyes to call me, you know. It's not like there's a time when I'm not watching you." His voice was booming right behind me. I glanced back. He was sitting next to Lydia.

Can they see you? I asked silently in my mind.

"Do they look like they can see me?" He frowned.

I glanced at Lydia. She looked up from her book and gave me a little wave, and then was engrossed in her book again. It was obvious I was the only one who could see and hear him.

"You seem to forget I can see *everything* you do," he said pointedly.

I knew exactly what he was referring to. He had seen me kissing Charles again. I gulped. I could feel my cheeks burning.

"What are we going to do with you?" Gabriel fumed.

Couldn't you have given me an ugly old man to help? I thought desperately.

"People of all ages are beautiful in God's sight!" he told me, a hint of anger in his voice.

Of course, they are! I agreed quickly (I was really blowing this. I wish Gabriel couldn't read my mind). Then, I grimaced. He knew about that thought too.

I looked back at Gabriel in frustration.

"It's all right." Amusement sparkled in Gabriel's eyes. "After all, you are human—sort of."

I wish I could be a perfect being like you. I'm just not, I thought.

"At least, you are trying." Gabriel's voice softened.

Didn't God know I might fall head over heels for Charles? Why was I put in a situation where I would be tempted so? I wondered.

"You always have the choice to obey God, regardless of the temptation!" Gabriel's voice thundered.

I almost felt the car vibrating with Gabriel's voice. I couldn't believe Charles and Lydia didn't hear him.

All right, I messed up. I let myself fall in love with him, and I shouldn't have. (If I had said this out loud, my tone would have been squeaky and small. I had blown it. Yet again!) *But please, Gabriel, don't take me off this case! I care about him! I want to help him until I can't anymore.*

"That's a truly unselfish thought. Congratulations! You are growing!"

Thank you, Gabriel! I am trying, I thought. I was definitely eating humble pie. I couldn't leave Charles yet, not when he needed me so much.

"Anyway, we are through attempting to keep you two apart. It's just not working."

So, Charles and I can stay together forever? I asked him silently.

"I didn't say that!" Gabriel said sternly. "I'm saying that you two can just enjoy your romantic moments from now on. It's useless trying to stop you. I give up!"

I'm sorry. It's impossible for me to stop loving him now.

"Believe me; I am aware of that."

My cheeks turned red as I looked down. *Gabriel, I know I disobeyed God. Could you please tell Him I'm sorry and ask if He'd forgive me?*

"God already has. All you had to do is ask." Then he started to fade away.

Thank you, and by the way, Gabriel, one last favor before you go. Could you please tell me where to find Charles' and Lydia's father?

He whispered the words into my mind.

Chapter 38

Several minutes later, after I had repeated the directions to Charles that Gabriel had given me, we parked in front of an old Victorian mansion. It had large white columns on a front porch that stretched from one end of the house to the other. The front yard was overgrown with weeds, and branches were strewn everywhere. Several shutters were dangling by nails, and some had fallen off already. On the front door was a hand-painted sign that said, "*Clinton's Bed and Breakfast.*" However, the whole place looked like it had been abandoned for years. We knocked on the door but wondered if anyone was even there.

A middle-aged woman answered the door. Her thin, graying hair was pulled back severely from her face. The crinkles around her mouth and eyes deepened as she looked us up and down suspiciously.

"What do you want?" she asked in a low voice.

"Does my father, Clinton Montgomery, live here?" Charles asked.

"I don't believe you. He hasn't seen his children in years, and I am sure he doesn't want to see you now!" With that, the woman started to shut the door.

Lydia reached out and caught the door with her hand. "That doesn't matter! We want to see *him*!"

"Go away, or I'll call the police!"

"Go ahead! No policeman is going to keep a man's children from their father," Charles pointed out.

She frowned as she watched us through narrowed eyes. "I'll let you visit him for a few minutes, but there's really not much to see."

"What do you mean?" Lydia asked.

"You'll see soon enough," she snapped. "By the way, my name is Mildred Higgins. I've become his caretaker by default. No one else wanted to do it."

"Why does he need a caretaker?" Charles asked. "He's not that old."

"You'll see," Mildred said simply.

We all went inside. The house was dark. The furniture had all been covered with white sheets, and the curtains were drawn. There was also a musty odor as if it were a tomb.

"Wasn't this a bed and breakfast?" I asked.

"It was until Clinton got sick. No one has spent the night here for a very long time."

"I can see why," I said before I could stop myself. Who would want to stay in this dismal dump?

Mildred glared at me. "You shouldn't speak of things you know nothing about. I've taken care of him as best I could. I wasn't able to be his full-time nurse and run the bed and breakfast too."

"Of course not!" Lydia quickly said in a sympathetic voice. "No one would expect you to do all that! Could we see our father now?"

"If you must. Follow me," she turned and started climbing up a long flight of stairs. We followed her in silence, not knowing what we would see. Once she ascended the stairs, she led us down a long, dark hallway. At the end of it was a closed door. She took a key out of her pocket and turned it in the doorknob.

"You keep him locked up?" Lydia asked, shocked.

"Only for his own safety," Mildred snapped back.

We went inside. The air was stale and heavy. The curtains were drawn here too. The entire house was like a funeral home. The bedroom was pretty bare except for a night table with a telephone on it and a double bed. There was a small shape huddled in the middle of the bed.

At first, there was complete silence in the room. Then we heard raspy breathing coming from the covered form under the blankets.

"Clinton, you have guests," Mildred said in a mocking tone. "Wake up, Bright Eyes."

The breathing got a little softer, and then a low male voice called out, "What? Who's there?"

"They say they are your children. Have you ever seen them before?" Mildred asked.

The man slowly opened his eyes and tried to focus on us but was clearly having trouble. "I've never seen any of you before in my life! Who are you?"

"I'm Lydia, Dad, and this is your son, Charles," Lydia grasped Clinton's hand in hers.

"We've come a long way to see you, Dad," Charles said as he patted his father's shoulder.

"And I'm just a family friend," I smiled warmly. "You're right. You haven't seen me before."

Clinton gazed at us with glazed-over eyes. His gray hair was unkempt and in greasy strands, and he hadn't been shaved in several days. "I don't know any of you. I don't have any children. They're dead. And soon, I will be too."

He turned over in bed toward the wall and away from us. "Go away. I don't feel like seeing anyone today. Don't come back."

"Don't worry, Dad. We won't." Charles answered angrily and sauntered toward the door.

"Wait!" Lydia pleaded. "Something is wrong!"

"I'll say! We have a father who hasn't seen us in decades, and he couldn't care less!" Charles exploded.

"It's time for you to leave him in peace. Soon, it'll be time for his lunch and medicine," Mildred told us.

"Medicine? What's wrong with him?" I asked suspiciously.

"He's either got dementia or Alzheimer's disease. We haven't figured out which one yet," Mildred said quickly.

"Has he been diagnosed by a doctor?" Lydia asked.

"A doctor comes each week to evaluate him and adjust his medication if needed," Mildred explained.

"What medication is he on?" Charles asked.

"He is on a variety of medications. They keep him alive. Now, if you would go, I've got to attend to him," she said.

We all began to leave Clinton's room.

"Goodbye, Dad," Lydia turned to touch her father's hand one more time.

"Wait! Don't leave!" Clinton suddenly reached out for his daughter's arm. His eyes were wild and desperate. "Help me!"

"Please go. Don't worry. He gets worked up like this sometimes. It'll pass," Mildred tried to explain.

Lydia gently untwined her father's hand from around her arm. "Don't worry, Dad. We'll be back."

"Thank you," he whispered. Then his eyes rolled back, and he was sound asleep again.

There was nothing else to do but for us to follow Mildred silently down the stairs in a solemn line.

When we got to the front door, she turned to us. "I'm sorry you had a bad experience. You can now see there's no use in coming back. He'll never realize who you are."

"That doesn't matter," Lydia answered defiantly. "We know who *he* is."

"I'm the one who's been taking care of him all this time. I'm his power of attorney. I make all of his decisions. And I say, leave him in peace."

"All right, Mildred. Maybe you are right," Lydia said quickly. "We just thought we'd check on him, but this was only a stop on our trip. We never planned on staying a long time here."

"Good." Mildred looked relieved. Then she added, "I mean—it's best that way. Seeing you will only confuse and upset him."

"But we're his family," Charles shook his head in disbelief.

"He doesn't know that. Leave, and don't come back." Mildred then shut the door in our faces.

"That was rude," Charles said under his breath as we turned around and walked toward the car together. "So that's it? We never see him again, and he dies?"

"No, that's not it!" Lydia shot back. "Something is off with that woman. She couldn't wait to get rid of us."

"I agree! Our job here is not done. God did not bring us this far, only to say goodbye to your father. God has a plan!" I told them.

"Then what is it?" Charles asked.

"Frankly, I have no idea. But He'll help us figure it out," I told him. For the first time, I completely believed that was true because I knew God was with us, watching over us every step of the way.

Chapter 39

We decided to put all of our worries aside and attend church service the next day. I did not have any revelations from Gabriel during the night. I had expected to hear his booming voice in my dreams all night long, and I was a little disappointed, to say the least. The old me would have been worried, but now, I knew I was never truly alone.

We all got ready, and then Charles drove us to the church in Carthage that was just a couple of blocks off the town square. It was a beautiful building with white clapboard and big windows on each side. It had a tall steeple with a cross at the top on the front end.

A friendly-looking man with thick salt and pepper hair stood at the top of the steps with his hand outstretched, welcoming people and shaking their hands as they went in. He smiled when he saw us looking up at him.

"Hello, there! You must be visitors! We're so happy to have you here! Come on in! What are your names?" he asked warmly.

Charles introduced us all to him and told him that he and Lydia were the children of Clinton Montgomery and that I was a friend of the family.

The man's name was Jonathan Stanley, and he was the preacher there. A cloud came over his kind face when Charles mentioned Clinton Montgomery's name.

"Yes, he and I were very close. He's the best friend I ever had in my life. I haven't seen him for about five or six months now. He never leaves his house. And when I went to check on him, Mildred, his caretaker, said he didn't want to see me. Could you please tell him I miss him?" Jonathan asked.

"Of course—if we get to see him again," Charles said.

"What do you mean?" Jonathan asked.

"Mildred said he might have dementia or Alzheimer's disease.

He was very confused and really out of it when we saw him. She said we shouldn't come back."

"That couldn't be right!" Jonathan shook his head. "Just six months ago, we were going fishing and doing church work together. He loved coming with me to visit some of our sick and shut-in members. He was vibrant and full of life. I wish you could have seen him then. Could I come with you to visit him? Maybe, I can help in some way," he offered.

"Of course," Charles answered. "Clinton may need you more than you know."

We went in and sat down on one of the pews in the auditorium. We sang "No Tears in Heaven," "Never Grow Old," and "Sing and Be Happy," among others. It was such a treat to hear and sing some of my very favorite gospel songs.

Then Jonathan delivered a fantastic sermon about reaching the lost and showing God's love to them. After the sermon, he made the announcements. Jonathan had us stand up since we were visitors and introduced us to everyone. Then, one of the elders led the closing prayer.

After the service, we found ourselves surrounded by friendly Christian members. Everyone wanted to meet us. There were sweet little old ladies, families, and young people lined up to introduce themselves to us. It was almost like we were celebrities. They were the friendliest congregation I had ever met. We felt so loved.

One girl stood out in the crowd because she looked very sad as she walked toward us. She was in her early twenties and had long thick brown hair that reached halfway down her back. She was pale, and her face had a delicate doll-like prettiness. She gently touched my arm.

"So, you are the long-lost family of Clinton Montgomery?" she asked softly.

"Well, I'm just a close family friend, but Charles and Lydia are his family," I explained.

"I must warn you, or Clinton will die soon!" The girl said.

Something inside told me she was deadly serious. That was probably why Gabriel had not come to me last night. God had sent this girl to us instead.

"Will you wait here just a moment?" I asked. "Let me get Charles and Lydia. They need to hear this."

I caught the attention of them both and motioned for them to come over. It took them a while to wade through the crowd of people, but soon they were at my side.

"What is it? You look worried," Lydia said.

"Listen. I think she has something important to tell us," I nodded toward the girl.

"My name is Rachel, and I've come to warn you about Mildred Higgins. She killed my father, and she'll murder yours too if she has the chance!"

"What do you mean? What happened?" Charles asked.

"My father was recovering from heart surgery when Mildred came to live with us. She was his nurse. I had to work two jobs to pay all the bills while he recovered. The doctors said they expected him to make a full recovery, and I was glad because he was all I had."

Rachel's eyes glistened with tears.

"But the longer she stayed, the faster my father went down. He became delirious, and soon he wouldn't eat. He got thinner every day, and the doctors had no idea why. I trusted Mildred to take care of him. I blame myself for it. I let her kill him!"

"No! It's not your fault!" Lydia shook her head. "You couldn't have known."

"If I had known, I would have been tempted to kill her myself!" Rachel's face was dark with anger.

"He finally died, which didn't take but a few months with her there. That's when we discovered a new will. It left her $25,000 for her 'excellent' care of him.

"My father wasn't rich. That was a big chunk of his estate, but this new will was ironclad with witnesses, and it had been notarized. I never had any idea when he did that because I was gone all the time, working as hard as I could to pay for his medical care.

"Also, in the will, he gave instructions for his body to immediately be cremated upon his death because it was cheaper. He didn't want me to pay for anything more expensive, like a gravesite.

"But years ago, when my mother died, we had buried her in the beautiful cemetery next to our church. Dad told me he wanted to be buried next to her someday. He never said a word about being cremated."

"All of that sounds very suspicious," Charles commented. "But did you ever find any evidence?"

"The day he was cremated, Mildred was moving out of our house. I was taking the trash out, and I happened to see a bottle of Laudanum that was almost empty. That was not one of my father's heart medications, and there was no reason for it to be there.

"I asked Mildred if my father had been taking it, and she immediately got angry. She said she had done the best she could to take care of him, and she had thought that would take away some of his pain.

"By this time, I was furious too, and I accused her of drugging him to death. I will never forget how she got up in my face and kind of sneered and said, 'You'll never be able to prove anything! Your father's body was cremated today, and he was on all sorts of medications when he died. You should be happy for him. He's out of his pain now. And you don't have to work two jobs anymore to pay for his care.'

"I told her I'd tell everything to the police, but she laughed and said they'd never believe me. I put the bottle of Laudanum in the kitchen cabinet and called the police. A sergeant said he'd be there the next day. She watched me and then slammed the door and left.

"I was able to sleep that night because I knew I'd be able to avenge my father's death. However, by the time the policeman came, that bottle had disappeared. She must have still had a key to our house and then came back and stole it during the night. That was the only piece of evidence I had. Without it, even the policeman didn't believe me." Rachel looked at us intently. "I'm telling you this now, so the same thing won't happen to your father."

"He did seem drugged when we saw him," Lydia commented.

"Then you don't have much time. It may already be too late!" Rachel warned us.

"Not if we go now!" Charles said. "Rachel, can you come with us? And tell Jonathan Stanley everything too, and get him to come with us. We need all the help we can get!"

Rachel ran over to the preacher and quickly told him everything. Then he walked toward us with an alarmed expression.

"I knew something was wrong. We've got to save him!"

Rachel got in the back seat with Lydia. Jonathan followed us in his red pickup truck. We all started speeding in the direction of Clinton Montgomery's house. Charles' knuckles were white as he gripped the wheel, turning down one street after another as fast as he could.

"Charles, it's going to be okay," I tried to reassure him.

"He's my last living parent, and I don't want to lose him," he said quietly. "I blame myself. I should have never left him the first time we saw him."

"You couldn't have known. I didn't even know. I only thought Mildred was a mean, cranky lady, not a killer."

"Just pray for us," Charles said. "Pray that it's not too late!"

Chapter 40

After what seemed like forever, Charles slammed the brakes to a stop, and we all got out and ran toward the house. I looked up and saw the curtains suddenly close in the window of Clinton's room. She was up there watching us and waiting for us.

Charles bounded up the front porch steps with all of us behind him. He beat on the door.

After several minutes that seemed like an eternity, we heard the door creak open a bit.

"What do you want?" Mildred snarled. "I thought I told you never to come back!"

"Where is our father?" Charles demanded.

"Where he was when you saw him last time!" Mildred said hatefully.

"We want to see him now! And by the way—" Charles paused, "You're fired!"

"You can't do that! You're not the one who hired me. He did!"

Rachel stepped forward and glared at Mildred. "It's over, Mildred. You're not killing anyone else!"

Mildred suddenly slammed the door shut, and we heard a click as she locked it.

"What do we do now?" Lydia asked.

"We're getting in there! No matter what!" Charles shouted. "Jonathan, come help me!"

Jonathan and Charles picked up a huge branch from the front yard and started ramming it through the front picture window. There was a sound of shattering glass. Then we all scrambled to get inside. We had to be careful not to cut ourselves on the broken shards of glass everywhere.

The inside was still dark and had the same musty odor as before. Charles raced up the stairs, taking several at a time. Jonathan was right behind him. We were following them. We all dashed down the long dark hallway, only to find that Clinton's room was locked.

With the strength of several angry men, Charles slammed the full force of his body twice against the door, and it burst open.

There Mildred was, on the bed beside Clinton, holding a knife to his throat. His eyes were open but hazy and bloodshot. It was apparent now that he was heavily sedated.

"I'll kill him now, so help me!" Mildred seethed. "You had to come back, didn't you! You thought you were so smart, checking up on me again! Well, the last laugh is on you! You are the ones ending up with a dead father!"

"Mildred, you're going to jail! But why don't you stop with one murder instead of two?" Rachel pleaded.

"You think this is only my second murder? I've had a lifetime career of murders! And I never got caught!"

"Until now!" Charles added. Then in a move so fast we could barely see it, he raced across the room, jumped onto the bed, and grabbed her wrist that held the knife. He shoved his father off the bed, away from her. Clinton lay in a crumpled heap next to the window. Lydia ran to him and held him in her arms.

Charles wrestled Mildred off the bed and onto the floor. She tried to stab him, running the knife up his arm and leaving a bloody gash. We could still hear Mildred shrieking hysterically—and then there was an eerie silence.

We rushed to the corner of the room where Mildred and Charles were. There Mildred lay, a grisly smile curling her lips. The knife was stuck through her stomach, all the way down to the handle. Her long gray dress was already soaked with blood. She had landed on the knife when she and Charles were struggling on the floor.

Jonathan knelt beside her and put his fingers to her throat to check her pulse. Then he said what we all knew. "She's dead."

"If she wasn't, soon our father would be!" Charles said as he got up. Mildred's blood was all over his clothes, and his arm was bleeding from her knife attack.

"It's a good thing Rachel and I came. We are witnesses that Mildred's death was an accident and that she was trying to murder your father," Jonathan commented.

"I'm glad you got the happy ending with your father that I never got with mine," Rachel said softly. Tears were in her eyes as she smiled.

"All Christians have happy endings," Jonathan told her. "Why he's up in paradise right now, having the time of his life! He's young again and out of pain. And if he could, he'd tell you never to worry about him again because he's happier in paradise than he ever was on earth." Jonathan patted Rachel's shoulder reassuringly.

"Thank you," she replied. "I'll remember that."

"We'd better call the police—and the hospital!" I reminded them.

"Why? She's already dead," Rachel said.

"We have to get our father to the hospital fast. There's no telling what all she's been drugging him with!" Lydia said.

Jonathan tried the phone in Clinton's room, but it was dead. It was apparent then that Mildred had disconnected the phone in his room so that he could never call for help. He had been a prisoner in his own home.

Since Mildred was dead, she was most likely in hades, paying for her lifetime of sins. Right now, she was probably already sorry, but it was too late for her to be saved.

We went downstairs to use the phone there. In a matter of minutes, the policemen and ambulance arrived. Mildred's covered corpse was carried away on a gurney. A medic patched up Charles' arm. Clinton was transported to the hospital, alive but unconscious.

The policemen asked questions about Mildred's death, but because there were so many witnesses, they quickly came to the conclusion that it was an accident.

We were all about to leave the dark house and stop by the hotel so Charles could change his bloody clothes. Then we planned to go out to a nice restaurant and celebrate. As we were about to walk out the door, the phone rang.

"Hello?" Charles said as he answered the phone. Then I watched while his face grew deathly pale. "Okay. We'll be right there."

"What?" I asked after he hung up the phone.

"Mildred may have won anyway. That was the hospital. Our father may die tonight!"

Chapter 41

Charles drove Lydia and me to the hospital in stony silence. We were all in shock. We had thought saving Clinton from Mildred would solve everything. It was horrible to think that our rescue of him may have come too late.

Jonathan was following us in his truck. He said he couldn't leave us until he visited Clinton in the hospital. He also wanted to pray with us for him to live.

Since there was nothing else she could do, Rachel said she'd be praying for us and had called a friend to drive her home. It was nice to already have Christian friends here that cared about us. We didn't feel so alone.

Charles parked the car at the hospital, and we all went in together. The girl at the front desk told us where Clinton was. We went up one floor and down several hallways to find him. The doctor was there waiting for us, looking grim.

"Hello, there. I'm Dr. Keller," he said. He shook our hands. "I want to warn you that we don't know if Clinton will make it through the night. The labs from his blood work are still pending. We suspect he has been poisoned with laudanum and maybe even arsenic. It's a miracle he's not already dead."

"Arsenic? That devil! She may have succeeded in killing our father, just like she wanted!" Lydia's fists were gripped tight.

"We are pumping his body full of fluids to wash out the toxins. We are also giving him nourishment intravenously. Still—it may not be enough," Dr. Keller said.

"Can we stay with him during the night?" Charles asked.

"Of course. Knowing you are here and that you care may make the difference between life and death," the doctor said. Then he left us alone with Clinton.

His thin, tired body lay there in the midst of tubes, wires, and machines. His face had a gray pallor, and he already looked dead. Only God could turn a situation like this around.

"We have to pray! It's up to God now," I told Charles and Lydia. Jonathan nodded in agreement. We knelt around Clinton's bed and begged God to bring him back to us. Mildred must not win! Hours slowly ticked by while we took turns praying. Around 4 a.m., we were all tired and drained. Jonathan had gone home but said he'd be praying for him throughout the night. Lydia and I were provided cots to sleep on. After stretching out in a recliner, Charles finally nodded off.

My eyelids were heavy, and I quickly fell asleep too. For a while, there was only a dreamless peace. Then Clinton and Gabriel appeared to me from paradise in a vision. Clinton looked just like Charles. His hair was thick, dark brown, and shiny, and his silvery-blue eyes sparkled when he saw me.

"Thank you for trying to save my life," he said.

"Looks like I didn't succeed if you're already up here," I answered.

"Oh, you succeeded. I'm more alive now than I've ever been. I'm young again. I have no pain." His face was radiant—what a difference from the thin, old man lying in the hospital bed.

"Clinton, you must go back. Your children need you!" I pleaded.

"They have you. They'll be all right."

"Clinton, you need to stay with your children. They've needed you all of their lives. They just didn't know it."

"Katie!" Gabriel's commanding voice filled the heavens as he glared at me. "There is only so much history you are allowed to change. This is his time, and he must decide for himself whether he stays or not!"

"Clinton, come back," I whispered. They soon faded from my eyes. "Come back," I begged. Then my eyes opened. I could hear the loud beeping as machines were going off. Nurses started rushing in, and then three doctors were there too, all shoving tubes in and out and trying to bring him back to life. Charles and Lydia had already been awake for several minutes before me. Now they were watching in horror, in slow motion, as their father lay dying.

Finally, Dr. Keller pulled the tubes out of Clinton's mouth, and his hand rested briefly on Charles' shoulder.

"It's too late. I'm so sorry," he said.

"No! It can't be!" Lydia cried. She had tears streaming down her face.

We were all gathered around Clinton's bed crying. It was over. I didn't know how Charles and Lydia would ever get over their father being murdered like this.

Suddenly, the machines started beeping again. I looked up from my tears. Clinton opened his eyes.

"I came back," he whispered in a weak voice.

"I don't believe it. He was clinically dead! I know he was!" Dr. Keller's face was puzzled. Clearly, he had never seen a case like this before.

"It's a miracle!" Lydia said through her tears.

"Dad, you're alive!" Charles exclaimed as he gripped his father's hand.

"I couldn't leave you again! We've already lost so much time. I was in paradise, and I saw you down below—yet so far away, grieving for me. I knew I had to come back." Then Clinton looked up at me. "And I remember you too. Thanks for talking some sense into me."

"Any time," I answered.

"It's tempting to stay once you are there. I never knew a place could be so perfect and peaceful."

"Thank you for coming back," Charles told him.

"I think I'll be here for a while now with you, my dear children." Clinton gazed up at Charles and Lydia and smiled.

"I've never seen anything like this in my entire career!" Dr. Keller commented, shaking his head. "I just don't understand!"

"It's called a miracle, and God did it!" Lydia told him.

I looked back from the doctor to Clinton. Gabriel was standing beside his bed, his arms folded. It was obvious only I could see him. He smiled at me.

Please tell God I said "thank you," I told him silently in my mind.

Out loud in words only I could hear Gabriel replied, "He said 'you're welcome.'"

Chapter 42

The blood work from Clinton's labs revealed days later that Mildred had indeed been trying to murder him. There were large amounts of laudanum and traces of arsenic in his system.

She had obviously just started him on the arsenic though, probably after she met us. She wanted to kill him before anyone could save him, and he had the chance to recover. Otherwise, he would have changed the will she had plagiarized, which gave her all of his estate.

The doctors kept predicting Clinton would have long-term side effects from being drugged and poisoned. However, Clinton continued to prove them wrong by getting better every day.

Charles and Lydia were enjoying getting to know their father better. He had an easy laugh like Charles', and his silvery-blue eyes sparkled with intelligence like those of his children. He constantly told Lydia and Charles how much he loved them.

All their lives, Lydia and Charles had thought that Evelyn, their mother, had left and taken them with her because Clinton had been an abusive monster.

However, that couldn't have been farther from the truth. Evelyn had mental issues, probably schizophrenia. Clinton had been trying to get her into a facility, so she could get treatment. They argued about it because Evelyn didn't want to go. So, one night, when Clinton was asleep, she packed up the kids and left.

The next day, Clinton woke up to an empty house. He drove all over town, searching desperately for them, but they were nowhere to be found.

He called the police. He used all of his money, hiring private detectives to find his family, but to no avail. For years, he lived on almost nothing and worked around the clock to pay for private detectives.

At Christmas, Clinton would think, now Charles is ten and Lydia is seven. He wondered if they were okay, if someone was taking care of them, or if they were even alive.

It grieved him to know that after Evelyn died, Lydia and Charles had been left to fend for themselves in orphanages and foster homes. Clinton would have given anything if he had gotten the chance to raise them.

There were a lot of tears shed when Clinton and his children realized what they had missed. Yet, they also knew what a gift it was to be reunited now and have the chance to finally be a family again.

People from all over town came to visit Clinton: little old ladies with yummy smelling casseroles, Jonathan—Clinton's best friend, and families with children to whom Clinton had given candy and gum in church.

Clinton was very popular and well-loved in Carthage. Apparently, everyone had been very worried about him during the last several months, when he had seemed to drop off the face of the earth.

Because the townspeople loved Clinton, they loved Charles, Lydia, and me as well. Soon, they knew us all by name. It felt so nice to belong somewhere and to be loved.

So, it should have been no surprise when Lydia brought in the Sunday paper, and there was a picture of the three of us on the front page. The headline read *The Heroes Who Saved Clinton Montgomery's Life.*

"Can you believe this?" Lydia asked, her face flushed with excitement. "We're famous!"

"Yeah, it looks that way," I slowly replied. I could already feel the blood draining from my face. "We're easy to find now. Time is ticking, and the mobsters are coming!"

"Oh, Katie—we're safe here. They wouldn't still be looking for us." Lydia shook her head with a reassuring smile.

"You don't understand. That was their job. Those two henchmen were supposed to either recruit Charles into being a killer like they were or take him out."

Charles came down the stairs. He was smiling and looking handsome in a navy-blue suit, ready for church. I hated to ruin his carefree mood.

"Charles," I called out to him as I handed him the paper. "We made the front page."

He surveyed the headlines. "Wow! I don't even know when they took that picture! We look pretty good, don't we?"

"Charles!" I snapped. "That's not the point! We've been discovered now! Those two criminals will be able to track us down!"

"Oh, Katie—you worry too much. It's been such a long time since we've even seen them. They're probably back in New York, murdering someone else by now."

"That's basically what Lydia thought. You and your sister really are alike!" I went up the stairs and slammed the door before saying something ugly that I would regret. Was I the only one who cared about their safety? I sat down on the bed, curled up my knees, and put my arms around them. I felt like crying.

"Having a human moment?"

I heard a deep voice behind me, knowing exactly who it was. There he stood, tall and gorgeous, with his arms folded. His eyes held a slight twinkle as he looked down at me.

"Oh, Gabriel! I'm tired of this gig! Why did God send me here if I can't save their lives? I know they are coming after us now! I can feel it! Charles and Lydia will die, and I will have failed!" Tears were flowing out of my eyes.

Gabriel was next to me in an instant. "Whatever happens now, you haven't failed." He put his hand on my shoulder, and I felt an instant feeling of peace and calm sweep over me. "Charles is a Christian now, but he used to be an atheist. You helped change him. You helped him rescue Lydia and reunited both of them with their father. So, to say you failed in any way would be inaccurate."

"Then why can't I leave now? I don't want to see them murdered!"

"Your assignment is not over! You are right to be concerned. Those two men are coming for Charles now! You'll have some difficult decisions to make in the near future. And I must warn you; you have a fully human body now. Anything that could kill a human could kill you. You must stay close to God and ask Him to protect you all."

I nodded. The image of Gabriel slowly faded into the air.

The feeling of calmness that Gabriel gave to me was quickly beginning to fade, and instead, his warning echoed in my mind... "Those two men are coming for Charles now!"

Chapter 43

I wiped away my tears as I heard a knock at my bedroom door. My room was getting a lot of traffic today. I had a feeling who my next visitor would be.

"Katie!" Charles quietly opened the door and let himself in.

I stood up and turned around. Right now, I didn't even want to look at him.

"Don't be angry. We can't be on the run for the rest of our lives." His hands grasped my shoulders.

Shaking them off, I turned around and glared at him. "I'd run forever if it would save your life!"

"Yes, I believe you would." His voice was soft, and his eyes looked deep into mine. "You love me that much." His face was close to mine now. It was easy to get lost in the smell of his cologne.

"I wish I didn't," I whispered.

"I know." His hands tenderly held my face and brought me closer.

I closed my eyes and forgot about everything else. He kissed me gently. I then felt his strong arms around my waist, gathering me to him. We held each other and enjoyed the love that was ours alone for the few short minutes we had stolen.

As long as I existed in heaven or on earth, I would never forget the way we loved each other. Sometimes you know in an instant when you've found the love of your life. I had known long ago he was mine and always would be.

Later that morning, we took Clinton back to church for the first time since he came home from the hospital. Jonathan hurried down the church steps when he saw him get out of our car. He walked toward us and patted Clinton on the back and shook his hand warmly.

"You're a sight for sore eyes, Clinton! Only you could survive a diabolical murder plot and arsenic poisoning!" Jonathan said cheerfully.

"Did anybody ever say you've got a warped sense of humor?" Clinton elbowed Jonathan. "Anyway, it really helps when a man's family and best friend break in and save him in the nick of time. Thanks, by the way," he grinned, looking like an older version of Charles. "If some crazy dame tries to poison you with arsenic, I'll return the favor!"

"Don't mention it," Jonathan replied. "It was fun."

As we walked toward the church, several women around Clinton's age came to flirt with him. They asked how he was doing and offered to bring him more food as he recovered. It appeared that Clinton was a local celebrity now, and he was definitely enjoying it.

After a few minutes, we gathered into the small chapel where Jonathan started his sermon about the Golden Rule; treating others as you would like to be treated.

I thought about how the world would be a completely different place if everyone actually followed that rule. There would be no more wars, murders, or crimes, just people living together in peace and happiness.

Even Charles' situation would be resolved. The two thugs wouldn't be after him. He'd probably still be running his successful limo business in New York and dating Angelina.

But then Charles and I would never have met. I could no longer picture my own existence without ever having him in it. Yet, I knew it was best for him if I left soon. He deserved a normal life with someone who wasn't already dead.

Jonathan concluded the sermon. We sang more of my favorite beautiful hymns. For a small congregation in a tiny town, they sounded like a chorus of angels to me. There were a couple of women with soaring soprano voices who hit high notes of which I could only dream.

After the final prayer, the mayor of Carthage, Mr. Craig Tomlinson, stepped up to the podium to make an important announcement.

"As most of you know, one of our favorite and most prominent citizens of our town, Clinton Montgomery, has been a prisoner in his own home for the last several months. He was drugged and nearly poisoned to death.

"Then, his long-lost son and daughter, Charles and Lydia, and family friend Katie broke into his house and fearlessly rescued him!" The mayor's booming voice filled the room.

"Charles, Lydia, and Katie are the kind of citizens we want and need in this town. They risked their lives to save another. They broke into Clinton's home to rescue him, not knowing if they would survive. They helped him escape from a madwoman. Clinton Montgomery would most likely be dead right now if Charles, Lydia, and Katie had never come to our town." There was not a sound in the room, as everyone listened in rapt attention.

"Therefore," he continued, "we would like to have a special ceremony Friday night for these three heroes. They will each be awarded a sterling silver key to our city of Carthage. They will always be welcome here and celebrated for their bravery."

The congregation seemed excited to hear this announcement. I glanced up at Charles and Lydia. They both looked down shyly, their faces red with embarrassment. It was clear that they didn't think of themselves as heroes, and I never thought of myself as one either.

The real hero in all this was God. He led us to Clinton Montgomery and then protected us as we worked to save his life.

After everyone was dismissed, we found ourselves surrounded by church members, shaking our hands and hugging us. We felt so loved and honored.

By the next day, our smiles had faded. I had gotten the newspaper that was thrown in our yard. I opened it to find a new picture of Charles, Lydia, Clinton, and me on the front page together. The headline was *Heroes in Carthage: A Story to Remember.*

It detailed again how we rescued Clinton from being poisoned to death. It also gave upcoming details about the celebration, where we would be presented with keys to the city.

Most importantly, though, it mentioned Charles' and Lydia's last name and where we were staying.

If Bruno and Jake were paying any attention at all, it would be no time before those creeps found us again!

Chapter 44

It would have been so easy to stay in Carthage forever. Clinton was healing faster than his doctors predicted. He already looked twenty years younger than when we first saw him, all drugged up. He now had a sparkle in his eyes and a spring to his step. It was clear that being around his two children had reversed the years and given him life once more.

He told Charles and Lydia that he wanted to open his large home to be a bed and breakfast, as he had before. He asked if we could help him fix it up and get it ready for business. Against my wishes, Charles and Lydia agreed to help him. If it had been up to me, we'd all be out of there by now. Then, the henchmen would never be able to find us.

Clinton owned several houses around town that he rented out to people. He said that Charles and Lydia could each pick out one of their own to live in. That meant they could easily have a future in Carthage and stay there the rest of their lives.

If only those hired guns weren't still scouring the countryside for us, life would have been happier, but there was always that shadow hanging over us. We knew that whatever joy we had could be snatched away in the blink of an eye.

As a distraction, we threw ourselves into helping Clinton fix up his house again. Lydia and I washed all of the curtains, did a lot of cleaning, as well as some redecorating. We went downtown and picked out pretty homemade quilts for the beds. Charles painted the dingy walls inside a bright, cheery white.

We worked hard and kept ourselves busy. It would have been easy to forget disaster was fast approaching Friday night, but I couldn't.

Friday morning, I decided to make one last-ditch effort to save Charles' and Lydia's lives. I got ready quickly and walked down to Charles' room to catch him before he started his next project around the house. If I had my way, he and Lydia would leave town today! It was the only way to keep them safe.

I knocked on the door.

"Come in," he answered.

I opened the door and found him sitting on the bed in his jeans and a white T-shirt. An open Bible was in his hands. He closed the passage he was reading and looked up at me.

"I knew you'd come. I was expecting you." He looked up at me and grinned.

"Charles, we've got to get you and Lydia out of here today! That ceremony is not safe with that crowd of people! You know those goons are still looking for you!"

"I know, and I don't care!" He shook his head in defiance. "I believe in the God you taught me about. If I die, I will be with Him and you for all eternity. And if you ask me, that's better than being alive in this rotten world!"

"I didn't stay with you this whole time in order for you to give up!" I said through clenched teeth.

"I'm not giving up!" he answered. "I'm giving in. I'm trusting God with my life. Isn't that what you wanted all along?" He got up, and in an instant, he was right next to me. His hand was on my shoulder, but I jerked it away.

"I want you to live!"

"Living without you, I'd be dead anyway. I'd welcome a bullet if I could spend eternity with you!" His voice was soft, endearing.

"Somewhere, along the way, I've failed!" I shook my head angrily. I turned around in disgust, ready to walk out the door.

"You didn't make me fall in love with you. I just did," he said.

I turned around, "Then why won't you listen to me and get out of here while we still can?"

"Because I'm not afraid of them anymore, Katie! If I die, I get to be with you forever."

Tears sprung to my eyes. He was ruining all of the plans I had made for him in my mind. I had wanted him to have a long, happy life, have kids and grandchildren one day.

He grasped my wrist and pulled me toward him.

"Don't cry, Katie. I never wanted to make you cry," he whispered. He pulled me toward him and slowly wiped my tears away with his fingers. He kissed my damp cheeks, where the tears had been. Then he lifted my face toward his and kissed me again. For a few moments, there was no danger, no henchmen, no anything but us. I always found an escape from the world when I was in his arms. After the kiss, I leaned my head on his chest, listening to the beat of his heart. He held me like that, against him, for several minutes.

"I'll never forgive myself if you die," I murmured.

"I'd rather die than live without you."

"If you refuse to leave, then I'll still go to the ceremony with you and Lydia tonight. And if those thugs show up, I'll do anything I have to, to save your life!"

"They don't have a chance with you there!" Charles grinned.

"I hope not!" I said quietly. I was worried, though. I should have been trusting God, but the human side of me was scared for him.

The rest of the day, Charles, Lydia, and I put the final touches on the house. We moved furniture around, opened the windows, and set fresh flowers out in a lot of the rooms. We stocked the freezer and refrigerator with a ton of great food for the upcoming guests.

Next week, Clinton's bed and breakfast would be ready to reopen. We gave Clinton a tour that afternoon of his refurbished home.

"I can't believe you all did so much work! It's like a new house," Clinton said with tears in his eyes.

"We did it just for you, Dad!" Charles said as he gave him a big hug.

"Won't you stay and run this bed and breakfast with me?" Clinton asked. "I've loved it in Carthage for years. I think you'd be very happy here. The people around town love you already, and I've been away from you and Lydia for a long time. We still have so much catching up to do!"

"Don't worry, Dad! We'll stay with you as long as we can!" Charles assured him.

"We sure will!" Lydia piped in. "I love this place already."

"And Katie—you stay with us too! You're already part of our family!" Clinton patted me on the back.

"Thank you! That's quite an honor!" I answered, not making him any promises that I would stay forever. I knew all too well I'd have to leave soon.

Later, Lydia and I were dressing up for the ceremony. I had on an A-line light-blue lace dress. She had on a long dress with sunflowers on it. She pinned some white flowers in our hair. We had fun getting ready together and talking. Lydia was already like a sister to me.

Charles was downstairs waiting for us. Our eyes locked as he gazed at me slowly descending the stairs.

"You look beautiful," he said softly.

"Thank you." I smiled back at him.

Then we all piled in Charles' car.

I wished to myself that we could have driven all night instead of going to the ceremony. However, the downtown square was just a few blocks away.

When we got there, I could already see a large crowd of people. Everyone from church was there, plus a lot of strangers. Charles parked his car next to the curb in front of the courthouse. There was a grassy area in the middle of the town square, where everyone was waiting for us. The people parted, and the mayor, Craig Tomlinson, eased through the crowd. He welcomed us, giving us each a warm, hearty handshake.

Then he led us to the middle of the crowd. I looked all around. I didn't see the mobsters anywhere, only the happy, welcoming faces of the kind townspeople. I looked up at Charles. He was already watching me with a slight smile on his face.

"See, you were worried for nothing. They aren't even here. Now, we can just enjoy the evening!" he said under his breath.

I nodded, suddenly feeling happy and carefree. I had been stupid to think the mobsters would follow us to a little town like this. Now I could relax!

Everyone got quiet as Mayor Tomlinson raised his hand to signal silence.

"We are gathered here tonight for a very special occasion. We are here to honor three new citizens of our town, Charles and Lydia Montgomery and Katie, their family friend. Their daring bravery resulted in saving the life of one of this town's finest people, Clinton Montgomery. For these past few months, Clinton been in declining health. Many of us missed seeing his smile around town. Several of us men missed his jokes and stories he used to tell when we'd get together at Molly's Donut Shop.

"Clinton was what I would call a good deed doer. He didn't know we knew that about him. In fact, he's probably embarrassed I'm even mentioning it now." Mayor Tomlinson looked over at Clinton and grinned. "When Mattie Gentle's husband died, Clinton quietly paid all of his hospital bills since they had no health insurance. When five-year-old Rhett Dillon needed a wheelchair after breaking his leg, Clinton was the one who got it for him. Anne Tillman came to town with nothing but the clothes on her back. A fire destroyed everything she had. Clinton paid the first several months' rent for her.

"I don't know what this town would do without citizens like Clinton Montgomery. And I didn't find out about any of the good deeds Clinton has done because he told me. He did them quietly—behind the scenes, but you all told me."

Clinton was looking down at the ground at this point with his face red.

"And now—" Mayor Tomlinson continued, "I want to talk about his children. The apple does not fall far from the tree with this family. When Charles and Lydia first saw their father again after years of being separated, Clinton was so far gone, he didn't know them. And they knew something was off with Mildred Higgins, Clinton's caretaker, who was literally drugging him to death.

"So, the next day, with Jonathan Stanley, Rachel Burns, and Katie, they broke into Clinton's home. Then they rescued him from the hands of a madwoman. Thank goodness they loved him that much, and thank God, we have him back with us now!"

There was loud applause. When it was quiet again, Mayor Tomlinson continued speaking.

"Now, we would like to honor our three new citizens by giving them each a key to the city. Whether they choose to stay forever or leave tomorrow, it's up to them. They will always be welcome here."

The crowd broke into applause once more. Mayor Tomlinson motioned for us to come closer with one hand. His other hand held our three silver keys. Lydia got hers first, and then Charles. I stepped up to get mine.

I could almost feel someone's eyes boring into the back of my head. I glanced through the crowd nervously and, at first, just saw a sea of happy faces. Then, I looked all the way to the back of the crowd. My breath caught. I saw them.

Bruno, the bigger, more sinister one, was staring straight at me. His eyes narrowed as an evil smile spread across his face. Jake, the smaller one, was right beside him.

I touched Charles' arm but then noticed he was already gazing at Bruno. Charles' eyes were steely and unafraid. He stood tall and proud, clearly unfazed by the presence of the mobsters.

I realized in an instant that this is what Charles had wanted all along, ever since falling in love with me. He must have known I'd be leaving soon, and if he was murdered, he could go with me!

I shook my head in disbelief and shock. I couldn't let him die just to be with me! He had his whole life ahead, whether I was a part of that or not.

I heard the click of a revolver. I looked back at Bruno, and he held a gun pointed straight at Charles. I wasn't the only one who noticed. The crowd saw him too, and pandemonium broke out. There were screams and chaos as people started running for cover.

Charles stood there, staring down the killers. Lydia and I were gathered on each side of Charles. Clinton and Jonathan were just a few steps away, staring in horror. Whatever happened, we'd go through it together.

Bruno held the gun aimed at Charles' heart as he walked toward us. "I just wanted to get a little closer, so I can get a clearer shot," he snarled. He knew he had us this time.

Charles shoved Lydia and me aside and stepped closer to Bruno. "I'll make it easier for you. You've got me now, Bruno. Do what you want."

"Giving up so easily?" Bruno was skeptical and seemed almost disappointed that Charles wasn't putting up a fight this time.

"No. I'm just unafraid."

"Why not?" Bruno clicked his revolver again, ready to shoot.

"God is on my side!" Charles declared in a steely voice.

"Good. Because you are about to see Him now!" Bruno pulled the trigger.

"No!" I shouted. I ran forward as I heard the explosion of the gun. I quickly ran in front of Charles, not thinking about what I was doing. I just knew I couldn't let him go.

I felt the bullet blast through my chest and then a pain so burning that it took my breath away.

And then there was nothing but peaceful blackness as I started to float toward a light. I saw Charles as he held my body in his arms, his shoulders shaking with sobs.

He would be okay, I thought. At least, he was alive.

Chapter 45

"Well, here you are again!" Gabriel said in mock disbelief, his huge arms crossed. "You sure are getting in a bad habit of dying all the time!"

"I had no choice this time! I had to save him!" I protested.

"You did have a choice," Gabriel paused, "and you made the right one!"

"I did?" I asked, confused.

"Giving your life for another is the greatest love of all. Just as Jesus did," Gabriel said.

"Anyone would have done what I did," I protested.

"If only that were true, the world would be a better place!" Gabriel declared. "Don't you see how you've grown? You were willing to put yourself in harm's way in order to save Charles' life. Before, you cared only about yourself."

"Thanks for reminding me."

"Now, you are the kind of person who belongs here!" I could see the beauty of heaven in his face.

"Really?" I asked eagerly, a smile spreading slowly from ear to ear. Then I remembered who I was leaving behind. "Gabriel, do I have to go just yet?"

He gazed down at me. "You really love him, don't you?"

"More than I ever thought possible."

"You won't have any special power."

"I don't care, as long as I can have him."

"We usually don't allow this," Gabriel said sternly. Then his voice softened. "However, rules are made to be broken."

"Thank you!" I whispered.

"I'll see you again in a little while. Seventy years are like a day to us up here."

"Goodbye, Gabriel. I'll miss you!"

"Oh, I'll be watching. We're closer than you think."

Gabriel's voice was fading, as was the outline of his face. I must be crazy for turning down the chance to go to paradise right now and see my family again. Nevertheless, I would see them soon enough.

I felt the wind blowing as I floated through the darkness. I had no idea where I was going, but I knew the general direction. I was unafraid, knowing that God held me in the palm of His hand.

Suddenly, I felt gravity taking hold of me as my soul entered my body again. There was still darkness about me, quiet and peaceful. Maybe, I was still dead.

And then I heard his voice faintly as if calling me from far away.

"Katie! Come back to me, if you can!"

My eyelids felt like heavy bricks as I tried unsuccessfully to move them. I then tried to move the rest of my body, but nothing happened. Two seconds back, and I was already having frustrating human issues.

I squeezed my hand and was surprised to feel my hand being squeezed back. Suddenly, I opened my eyes.

"Charles!" My voice was weak and faint. It didn't even sound like me.

"Katie!" Charles had tears in his eyes as he gazed down at me. He looked awful like he hadn't slept in days. He had dark circles under his eyes, and his face was pale, but his eyes were shining. "I would have died if I had lost you!"

"I know. I felt the same. That's why I had to come back!" My voice was starting to get stronger, but I still felt like I had been run over by an eighteen-wheeler.

"They'll let you stay with me?"

"For the rest of our lives."

His hand was in my hair, and he lifted my head up a few inches and kissed me. I was starting to feel better already.

"Let's get married soon," he suggested, his voice husky.

"Oh yes," I said softly, "soon."

I lay back down, and my eyes closed into a happy, peaceful sleep. I dreamed of him.

Chapter 46

A few days later, Charles wheeled me out of the hospital in Carthage. There were cameras flashing, and a crowd was gathered all around us. Our story had gone national, and everyone knew who we were.

Reporters were asking questions and demanding answers. Charles ignored them and quickly pushed my wheelchair through them. Then, he lifted and put me into the car and got into the front seat.

Some of the reporters were tapping on the windows. Charles glared at them as he started the engine. When we drove off, the reporters looked frustrated as we left them in our dust.

"They are so annoying!" Charles fumed. "They've been here like hungry wolves ever since this happened."

"Can you blame them? Nothing like this has ever happened here."

"And hopefully, it never will again! What do you mean, jumping in front of me like that? Were you trying to be a hero?"

"I couldn't let you die—and you would have! Bruno was there to kill you that day!"

"I didn't care! If I died, I could be with you for all eternity. That's what I planned, anyway."

"Yes, I figured that out. You sure are stubborn!" He was starting to make me angry.

"Yeah, well, so are you! That bullet should have killed you. The doctors still don't know how you survived. They might as well have shot me too. I could never live without you, Katie."

I smiled. "Don't worry. You don't have to now."

Bruno and Jake were locked up in jail, hopefully for the rest of their lives, while on the other hand, Charles and I had a lifetime of happiness ahead. We had won because God was on our side.

When we got back to Clinton's house, everyone was outside cheering. The front yard was decorated with colorful balloons and

215

streamers. There were tables of delicious food. Jonathan was even grilling hamburgers for all of us. The smell of that beef cooking was making me ravenous.

"Hungry?" Charles asked as he saw me looking at the grill.

"*Oh, yeah!*" I answered. "There's nothing like a freshly cooked cheeseburger."

Charles carefully lifted me out of the car and then carried me toward our future family and friends. I leaned my head against his shoulder and smiled.

"Thank you, God," I whispered softly, and I felt peaceful and happy like never before. Whatever happened in the future, everything would be all right because God and Gabriel were watching over me.

Epilogue

I have slowly been recovering at Clinton's home, which is flourishing as a bed and breakfast. Our stories in the newspaper about the mob chasing us have really been great for business. It seems like everyone in this part of the country wants to spend two or three nights here now.

I've been really busy planning our wedding. Hopefully, it'll be in the next few weeks. One would think I'd be nervous and scared about getting married, but I can't imagine my life any other way.

Lydia will be my maid of honor, and Clinton will walk me down the aisle. If Charles is at the end of that aisle looking at me as I walk toward him, I know I won't be afraid.

When I think back over all that has happened since I died for the first time, I am amazed at how I have grown. God used every situation to help me change into the person I was meant to be.

I'll never be perfect, but I'm going to keep on reaching toward God for the rest of my life. I trust Him more than ever before and know that He'll always be by my side.

The End

CPSIA information can be obtained
at www.ICGtesting.com
Printed in the USA
BVHW011930141221
624046BV00007B/122